THE CHOICE

THE CHOICE

Finding Life in the Face of Death

Six Stories from
A Therapist's Casebook

JAN HATANAKA , Ph.D.

BASTIAN BOOKS

Published in 2008 by
Bastian Books
www.bastianbooks.com
A division of Bastian Publishing Services Ltd.

ISBN 978-0-9782221-8-5

Cataloguing in Publication Data available from Library and Archives Canada.

Cover image and design: Angel Guerra, Archetype
Text design and typesetting: Greg Devitt Design

Printed in Canada

*This book is dedicated to those who
unselfishly share their firsthand knowledge and
hard-won wisdom — by revealing their struggles,
they allow their humanity to shine as a
beacon of hope for all*

CONTENTS

ACKNOWLEDGMENTS

My thanks to:

Angel Guerra, a dear friend, for your full commitment in helping me move the book from concept to finished product. The process began when you said, "One day if we are lucky, we'll be given a second chance. And, in that moment, when time almost stops, then starts again, we'll find ourselves asking the most perilous of questions: How do I go on?" The late George Freemesser, physician, psychiatrist, priest, and mentor at the forefront of interdisciplinary studies. His words guided me as I worked on this book: "We are at our best when doing two things: learning and connecting with others." Don Bastian, my editor and publisher, for your genuine interest in this topic. Your dedication to the subject matter and to me personally have been of tremendous support.

My family, for grounding me in the knowledge that flexibility and determination are required to adapt to the circumstances of life. It was you who collected the pieces of who I was and who I am and gently handed them to me as I put myself back together again. In particular, I thank:

My husband, Bill, for holding me during those long days and very dark nights. It is with your ongoing love and support that I find the courage to continuously challenge myself.

My sister, Lauri, for reminding me of who I was, and working with me to help me become the person I want to be.

Bobby, for allowing me to see the strength of character that develops in those who must be counted on before their time.

Ryan-James, for teaching me how to graciously persevere no matter what life brings. I am continuously inspired by your optimism.

Abigail and Victoria, for teaching me what the human heart is capable of.

THE CHOICE

INTRODUCTION

This book is about our relationship with death: how it comes to us, how we run from it, and how we discover that it is part of who we are.

My own relationship with death is both professional and extremely personal. Ironically, after choosing a career in health care and specializing in palliative care and bereavement counseling, I encountered death firsthand through a stroke that nearly took my life.

Almost as devastating as the stroke itself was the fact that neither my own professional resources nor those of medicine, psychology, and theology could help me get over the fear of death that haunted me. I understand now, after twenty subsequent years of clinical and academic research, that a critical piece was missing from the models that I had been learning and teaching. While those who were terminal were encouraged to come to terms with the inevitability of death, those who were not terminal were encouraged to get over it. What was missing was the fact that death is not something we *can* get over. It is part of who we are as human beings. And once it reveals itself to us, we are faced with the most important choice of our lives: to try to find our way back to our former life of innocence by turning away from death, or to begin developing the skills we need in order to learn to live an authentic life knowing that death is real.

This book is about the futility of running from death and the necessity of giving death its rightful place in our lives. It shows in dramatic detail how we must wrestle with this choice.

No one escapes the choice. Sooner or later, death will come. It may come while we sit in a doctor's office; it may come by way of a phone call in the middle of the night; it may come when we glance across at a parent one day and realize that most of who they once were is gone.

I hope that by reading this book you will begin to recognize what you are up against. I hope you will understand that there is a way to walk with death — that the weight of knowing death will not crush you. You do not have to be on your own to do the learning. A process of learning to live with death is outlined in these pages. The specific steps come from the hardwon wisdom of those who have done it, people like you who were happily going about their lives when death imposed itself on them. I hope to demonstrate that learning to live with the reality of death can be accomplished by those who are willing to do the work.

Simply put, this book emphasizes the importance of acknowledging the inevitability of death as a significant catalyst to living a life of enhanced meaning. It invites you into real-life situations: my own story and those of five others, who are composites based on real-life stories from my casebook as a Grief Reconciliation Specialist. These stories show how, by learning to live with death, we can become truly free to live.

It may be helpful to state what this book is about and what it is not about.

For instance, this book is not a book about dying. It does not describe how to let go of the world when all hope of continuing to live is lost. There are many groups currently conducting excellent research in the area of palliative care. While it is important to examine the issues of those who are dying, it is equally important to assess the reality of death from the perspective of those who are living.

This book is about the process of gaining an awareness of death — and then integrating that awareness into our quest for life. It describes several of the ways that awareness of death enters our consciousness when we are in crisis.

This book is not about the sudden transformation undergone by a small percentage of people who have a Near-Death Experience. To the contrary, it is about the shocking normalcy of grief experienced by most humans at some point in their lives.

In fact, this book is not about an event at all but rather about a process, a sequence of interdependent stages that must be individually examined and understood before we can move forward to address significant issues.

These stages ultimately form the foundational cornerstones upon which a greater understanding of the larger issues around the reality of death can be built.

As you read the book, it will become evident to you that there are inadequacies in the way our current medical system and our psychological and theological communities mobilize to help those who must come to grips with the knowledge that death is real.

It is also critical to understand that this book is not about resolving grief or getting over death. It is also not about a relative ranking of an individual's right to suffer based on their particular circumstances.

Succinctly, this book is about reconciliation. It introduces a new process, one that I call the Grief Reconciliation Process. This process articulates the stages that are worked through by those who learn to live with death. The stages are **Surviving; Assessing** — Self, Others, God; **Depression; Epiphany of Despair; Acceptance;** and **Acquiring Resources** — Self, Others, God. Those who go through the process have to reconcile themselves to the work involved at each stage, and it is the process as a whole that helps them learn to live with death. As will be seen in the six stories, the process of reconciling grief leads to wisdom, understanding, and context in applying meaning to life.

The story **Intergenerational Grief** looks at how entire families can get stuck in a vicious cycle of grief. Even two generations removed from the death of a family member, grief-related problems may still exist.

Striving to Be Whole shows how physiological and psychological factors are only part of the recovery process. In order to more fully recover, we must commit ourselves to the arduous negotiation process of learning to live with death. Part of this negotiation involves the spiritual quest that we take on as we attempt to answer the big question, "How do I want to live, now that I know death lives at the core of who I am?"

Perceived Threat describes how awareness of death can come to anyone at any time. Far from being an end point, learning that death is real offers one the opportunity for a new beginning. Death can be a powerful teacher.

Intergenerational Wisdom highlights the relevance of death in healthy living. Death is a very important topic to older adults. In this story, an older adult creates a pathway for the younger generation of his family as they all learn about death as part of life.

Representing the Dead describes the Grief Reconciliation Process as it relates to the world of those who are bereaved. In it we see the process of coming apart, and the work that must be done in learning to put oneself back together again.

Alongside these five, I have also included my own story, **On the Bridge Between Life and Death,** which explores how futile it is to run from death.

This has been a difficult book for me to write. I am not used to speaking openly about my personal struggles. Why have I done so? Because I know what it feels like to be lost. To look at a blank sheet that bears no clues. To worry that you will never again feel well. And because I have discovered that learning to live with death is a critical component of healthy living. I have listened as many recovered people have described the path to health that comes by learning to live with death. I also know that to avoid describing this path would dishonor the people I have had the privilege of interacting with on the topic of death. It is their wisdom, combined with what I have learned on a personal, professional, and academic level, that I hope to share with you.

I am convinced that the information contained in this book will provide individuals and families with practical advice, offering them sustenance throughout their ordeal. It may also be helpful to caregivers who wish to enhance their understanding of the role of death as part of the recovery process.

This is not an easy book to read. It will challenge you to develop new skills. Learning to live with death requires a great deal of hard work. That said, should you decide to do the work, you will reap extraordinary benefits. Your newfound wisdom will allow you to become a guide for others.

By learning to live with death, you will understand how intimately we are all connected. If allowed, death itself can become the most positive and powerful of teachers.

THE GRIEF RECONCILIATION PROCESS

I.   Surviving
II. Assessing — Self, Others, God
III. Depression
IV. Epiphany of Despair
V.   Acceptance
VI. Acquiring Resources — Self, Others, God

- The dotted black circle reveals what can happen if one does not learn to live with death.
- The solid path reveals how one can learn to live with death — the Grief Reconciliation Process.

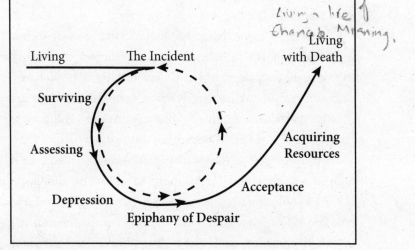

Living a life / Change b. Meaning.

A great deal of research supports the fact that many people never learn to live with death. The circular route depicts the path of a person caught in a circular pattern of grief, never able to reconcile the old life and the new. Rather than heading out in search of new learning, this person may become stuck in a self-destructive cycle of surviving, assessing, and depression, and back to surviving. This book explains how we can avoid this unhelpful pattern of grief.

The solid black path describes the six stages of the Grief Reconciliation Process. It describes how we can learn to live passionately within ourselves and with the world after having come face to face with death. It is this path that is the subject of this book.

The path will take you on a journey that has been mapped out by people who have learned to live with death. It is made up of the various steps that are necessary to integrate death into living. It is not an easy path. But those who have traveled it are witnesses to the fact that it is worth the effort.

I have superimposed these two routes so that you may see that the paths run parallel to each other for part of the journey. So much so that in the early stages it is hard to predict just who will have a successful recovery. When tragedy strikes, members of both groups must learn to depend on others — this is **Surviving**. It is difficult to hand oneself over in our culture of self-directed autonomy.

In the next step of the journey — **Assessing** — members of both groups begin to realize that things have changed. They begin to ask questions and to evaluate themselves, others, and God. The outcome of this investigation may not be good. **Depression** sets in for both groups of people as they digest the painful discrepancy between what is and what they hoped would be. Depression is a time that people describe as an all-consuming fear. They describe themselves as feeling very much alone.

It is at this point that the two paths separate.

Those who do recover move ahead in the process of recovery differently. They are not saved from the suffering that comes with knowing that all is not well. They stay with the suffering long enough to assess what is at the heart of the matter. We cannot control life. We cannot control death. Awareness of death is identified as a significant factor in the person's life. Awareness of death becomes a pivotal factor in their recovery. Instead of turning away from the truth, they learn to concede to the reality of death.

This is the stage called **Epiphany of Despair**. In it the truth about life is revealed, offering an exit ramp to recovery. In this stage, people learn to accept that there is little value in continuing to deny something that is undeniable. They conclude that despite the horror of this genesis, they have a choice to make: pretend that what they see is not true, or accept that death is real and learn to live differently.

In the stage of **Acceptance,** the question changes from "How do I get back to my old life?" to "How do I deal with the reality of death?" Acknowledging a desire to live despite acknowledging the reality of death encourages them to negotiate in an attempt to obtain the skills needed in order to continue to live: this sets the stage for them to learn to negotiate with self, others, and God. This is called **Acquiring Resources**. Through this integrated learning, they learn to live with death.

ON THE BRIDGE BETWEEN LIFE AND DEATH

My Story

The first time I was exposed to death, I did not learn what it had to teach me. Instead, I ran from it. That was all I knew how to do. Death was the enemy. To protect myself and my family, I was determined not to allow it a place in my life. The problem with running away from death was that the path I was on did not take me away from death and back to my old life. It led me around in a circle. After a great deal of time and energy, I ended up right back face to face with an enemy now more fearful than ever.

How I came to see running away from death as a futile exercise, how I learned to think strategically about bridging the chasm between death and life, and how I have learned to live a full and happy life I hope to share with you by telling my story.

It happened one fine day in the fall of 1985. I had spent the morning away from my job as a community health nurse in the city of Edmonton, Alberta, attending a lecture at the conference centre, close to where I lived and worked. When it was over, I had a nice lunch with several friends from the medical community who had also attended the lecture. Then, with no other appointments scheduled that day, I enjoyed the rest of the afternoon catching up on routine tasks in my office.

Then I drove the eighteen or so blocks to our apartment and went straight to the kitchen to make dinner. My husband came home at around 6 p.m. I was happy to see him. He had been traveling on business the previous two days.

At 6:30, we sat down to enjoy our meal together. At 6:45, my head began to shake. It was an odd feeling, one I would not be able to describe accurately until I experienced a minor earthquake while visiting Montreal a few years later. I looked over to my husband and noted that he did not look concerned. Being well versed in first aid, I thought that if I was going to faint, I should get myself to the ground. I slipped off my chair and put all my energy into finding the floor.

∘ SURVIVING ∘

According to my husband, I lay there looking very serene. He was anything but. He had just witnessed his wife of five years slip into an unconscious state. He knelt beside me and pleaded with me to open my eyes; to give him a sign that I was simply having a moment that would pass. When I did not respond, he took me into his arms (he is a former football player, and I am petite), got me into the car, and drove in a panic to the hospital a few blocks from our home.

Several hours later, I woke up in the emergency department. Everything looked dark, except for my husband's white shirt, which I could see out of the very corner of my left eye. A wave of sheer terror was interrupted by my husband's voice. He leaned over me so I could see the outline of his face and whispered, "Don't worry. I will take care of you." I believed him. I felt very grateful. Then I went back to sleep, leaving him to deal with the bad news, alone.

The news was that, at the age of twenty-eight, and five months' pregnant with our first child, I had suffered a major stroke. It was impossible to tell whether either of us — I or our baby — was going to make it. If I lived, it would be days before the doctors would be able to assess the neurological damage. If the baby lived, well, the variables were too numerous for anyone to make a prediction.

It was my husband who had to make the call to my parents in the middle of the night. It was he who sat at my bedside, shouldering the load alone until my mother flew in from Ottawa and joined him, twelve hours later. Together, they stayed with me day and night. They became my lifeline. They held me and I felt great comfort in their arms.

Together they worried, and I survived. Every once in a while, I would wake up, see my family, and go back to sleep. In those moments, I did not look to God for comfort. I did not pray. I did not care that I was being prayed for. I did not worry about what the future might hold. My needs were much more basic than that. I opened my eyes, I found relief in knowing I did not have to think, and then I closed my eyes again.

I would like to tell you that I fought hard, that I refused to take this adversity lying down, but the truth is, I did nothing but surrender myself to the care of others, trusting them to take charge. My body was in the shop. It was getting fixed. What would have happened if there had been no one for me to surrender to?

∘ ASSESSING — SELF, OTHERS, GOD ∘

Several days later, I began to wake up and take inventory of my situation. Only then did I begin to realize what I was up against. One morning, lying in my hospital bed, I tried to move. The right side of my body was numb. I thought it was dark but was told the problem was with my sight. I tried to ask questions and was unable to get the words out of my mouth in any kind of order. I asked about my baby. That is when my agony began. My family committed themselves to me even more deeply. They stayed with me both day and night.

I was torn between trying to push my loved ones away to protect them from the ugliness of the situation, and grabbing onto them because I knew that without them I did not know how to fight. I was angry with myself for not being strong enough to push them away. It was difficult to see them suffer, and yet I had more concern for myself than for them.

Over the next weeks, waves of panic continued to wash over me, but instead of drowning under the weight of them, I grabbed the lifelines being thrown to me. I turned to my family for their physical support and prayers, and to the doctors, who continued to reassure me that everything was going to be fine.

I focused on doing my part. I fought to concentrate: to try to remember, to move my body, to make my eyes see. Sometimes my body would comply; other times the circuits were jammed, and no matter how hard I tried, I could not get it to do what I asked it to do. My family worked right along with me. My parents divided their tasks: my mother stayed with us, while my father stayed at home in Ottawa to care for my two younger siblings. My husband became the director of my care. He made sure someone was with me at all times. He enlisted the support of a housekeeper and took our friends and neighbors up on their countless offers of help. Together, they circled around me. They walked with me and pushed me to keep challenging myself. Their support made it easier for me to be awake.

The weeks turned into months, with much of my time spent attending some sort of treatment session (with doctors, therapists, or spiritual advisors). These meetings were focused on two things: first, how to fix the problems I had, and second, how to keep something like this from ever happening to me again. Both seemed to be reasonable goals. The professionals told me what to do, and my family and I made sure I got it done. At the time, it was beyond my capability to think the problems through. So I simply did what I was told.

The conclusion of the many experts that my family and I consulted, and from the results of the hundreds of tests they had run, was that the stroke was a complete fluke; that nothing I had done or hadn't done had caused it; that the odds of anything like this happening again were next to nil. I can see the flaws in their thinking, but that is with the advantage of hindsight. At the time, it was wonderful news, and all of our attention turned to helping me get back to normal.

My baby became my lighthouse in the storm. I made a deal with myself and I bargained with God: If I could keep my baby, if my baby could be healthy, I would happily settle for whatever residual effects of the stroke I must experience. I would not complain.

Weeks went by and slowly my body began to heal. First my right arm regained some mobility, and then my right leg. The small slice of vision I had to the left in both eyes began to expand. Eventually I was blind in only half of both eyes, which made it possible for me to see what was in front of me.

My mind was not as quick to heal, however. The first time I ventured out of the house by myself was several months after my stroke. I felt ready to challenge myself and was sure I could make it around the block. But shortly after leaving our front door, I somehow got turned around. I found myself completely lost. Believe me, I tried hard to figure out where I was. I did what I had been taught to do: I searched for clues; I tried the relaxation techniques; I prayed.

As I sat on the sidewalk that day, I got my first real taste of humility. Eventually a woman came and knelt beside me and asked if I needed help. I cannot begin to tell you how powerful her gesture of kindness was to me. At that moment, I was completely dependent on someone I had never met before. Someone I would never see again. The woman helped and eventually I got home. I was so consumed by my own desperation that I did not think to thank her. What I did, instead, was crawl back into my little hole and hide. I decided to stay there until my baby came and life got back to "normal."

More months went by, with more hospital stays for tests and to monitor my pregnancy. My baby continued to grow. I prayed every day. I was grateful to God for having kept his part of the bargain. Finally, five months after my stroke, our perfect baby arrived. I no longer had the acuteness of mind I once had, and I still had only half my vision, but a deal was deal, and I was grateful that I had been clever enough to strike one. Life was perfect.

By this time, my mother had returned to her home. My husband and I set to work on our family life. We set up systems to compensate for the residual effects of the stroke. My husband, a man of great focus and determination, coached me through the trials that challenged me every day. Our baby was always next to me as I continued my therapies; our very own baby boy was making all of our efforts worthwhile.

Over time I learned how to get around without walking into things on my blind side. My husband made lists for me, and I learned how to follow them. He ran interference for me: his life and his skills kept things simple for me. He was out in the world competing. All I had to do was to love our baby and follow the straightforward instructions he left for me every day.

It was a simple life and we were happy. So happy, in fact, that we decided to have another baby. My health was improving. We had checked and double-checked with health-care professionals to see if there were any counter-indications. There were none. I became pregnant with our second child.

∘ BACK TO SURVIVING ∘

For the first several months of the pregnancy, all was well. I did not feel overly tired or sick. I was not burdened with stress. I went about each day enjoying my little boy and looking forward to giving him a brother or a sister. Then one day my husband got a call at work. Our family doctor had attended a conference where a paper was presented on a clotting condition that caused strokes. He asked my husband to bring me in for a blood test to rule out an underlying clotting disorder. He did. I did. And that is when things came crashing down again.

I did have a blood-clotting disorder: I could at any time experience another stroke. I had no idea what it meant to be strategic and to assess what I was up against. I simply looked for someone or something to blame. The health-care team did a wonderful job of joining me in that quest. There were as many theories as there were doctors. Some of the theories were directed toward my own pathetic body, others toward my genetically flawed family. The doctors did not know how to fix the problem while I was pregnant. If I lived through the pregnancy, they said, only then would they be able to design care that would keep me safe.

I handled all this by shutting myself down. Perhaps it was just too much for a mind that had not yet healed. Whatever the reason, I did not take in what they were trying to tell me. I did not fully understand that there was a problem with the way my blood flowed in my body and that my odds of having another stroke were high. I was like a child covering her ears and yelling in order not to hear something unpleasant.

My family carried the burden of those days. My mother came to stay with us again, until my husband was able to hire a full-time housekeeper to keep an eye on me while he was at work. On some level, I knew this stranger was there to keep our son safe in the event that I had a stroke or died, but I could not bring myself to think about it, let alone talk about it. So I simply did not. I got up every morning, I did what I had to do, I continued on with life. A simple life. A life with my young son and the baby who was yet to be born. I don't know how my husband managed to carry on his job in the financial industry weighed down by such a fragile home life. I wonder now how many others go to work every day with similar burdens.

Together, my husband and our families worried. As for me, I had in my mind that if my baby arrived, if I could make it through, the doctors would fix me and all would go back to normal. I set my sights on the finish line and did whatever it took to get there: the treatments, the tests, the visits to the hospital.

Finally, our second son was born. A few minor complications were easily overlooked. He was healthy. I was free to get back to my real life.

∘ ASSESSING, THE SECOND TIME AROUND ∘

The way I saw it, the health-care team had been strategic and the care I received had been top-notch. My hard work and prayers had paid off. I was feeling confident that God had heard me; that he had decided to allow me to be with my family. God had come through for me. I had beaten the odds. We had two beautiful babies. All these thoughts of death could finally be put behind me.

Physically, my health continued to improve, and with some ongoing help from a housekeeper and from both our families, I was able to care for our babies. There were many things I could no longer do with a mind that wasn't whole and vision that was only fifty percent. I could no longer be out in the world the way I once was—coordinating telethons, speaking at conferences, appearing at public functions with my athlete husband. I was no longer bold. Those days were gone. I would tuck myself into my home away from the scrutiny of the world and learn to survive. When I was out, I would take on only simple tasks that did not cause me anxiety or stress. I would not focus on the things I could no longer do; I would focus on the things I could: I could hold my babies. I could love my babies. I was so grateful to have them that every day was a joy. I dared not complain to anyone, especially God.

But when I sat alone, with my babies, an anxiety deep inside me would rise up. What if I had to leave them one day? What if I had another stroke and was not able to care for them? But I turned these questions off. I breathed in and prayed to God to keep his part of the deal. I lifted my babies up to him and thanked him for creating such perfect little miracles. I would prove to him that I was a good mother and that I deserved to live. In return, I would never complain about what I had lost. I would fight hard to live. I would continue to do all that the experts suggested. I would work as hard as necessary to learn how to manage.

Anyone who knew me then knows how thankful I was to have a husband who loved me and my two baby boys. Life was simple but good. I had been healthy, then unhealthy, then healthy to the point that I was beginning to feel confident that things would be okay. When I heard other mothers complain about getting up in the middle of the night to care for their babies, I smiled and thought of how much I loved hearing my babies call for me. My husband and I were grateful. We had done all the right things. Our hard work was paying off.

∘ BACK TO SURVIVING ∘

Then one morning, on an ordinary spring day in 1993, I bounced out of bed, ready to spend my waking hours with my boys. I walked into our en suite bathroom and crumpled to the floor. I do not remember falling. What I do remember is how comfortable I felt. It was a feeling like no other: a feeling of absolute peace.

After what seemed a long time, I was interrupted by the sound of my husband's voice. I did not want to respond to him, but I did. As I came back to life, I could hear his pleas, his cries. He was holding me in his arms and screaming at me to open my eyes, begging me to live. I looked at his face. I recognized the look of terror in his eyes. Only then did I realize that it had happened again.

∘ BACK TO ASSESSING — SELF, OTHERS, GOD ∘

The days following the second stroke were the most intense days of my life. Unlike the first go-round, this time I was wide awake. Certainly, I was grateful to be alive, grateful that the incident had not claimed any more of me than it had already taken. But while I underwent the tests and took the medicines and submitted myself to the prescribed treatments, I began to see that things were different.

I was frightened to the depths of my being.

It was becoming clear to me that my health crisis was not a temporary one. The stroke was not an accident. I did not have the personal resources to control something similar from happening. Those in the health-care field did not know how to fix me, and no supernatural occurrence was going to grant me reprieve from further trauma. I could not count on myself to outthink this problem. Deals with God could not be made. The people who took credit for helping me after my stroke were not going to save me.

In those very dark days, I began to assess things differently. I began to wake up and see that the road I had been on had not taken me to a new place: it had taken me around in a circle. It was as though I was lost in a forest and after walking for a very long time, I had ended up back where I had started years before.

For the first time I recognized the place where I stood: it was a place of fear. At the time, I could not describe where I was, but I knew I had been there before: off balance, uncertain, petrified to take my next breath. I had stood in that very spot and waited to hear that the situation was temporary, that if I would simply stay calm and do as I was told, everything would soon be back to normal. I had waited for the words, and when they came, I had grabbed hold of them.

This time I could see that the words were simply words. I tried to tell myself I had it wrong. I tried to believe the hopes and promises that everything would work out just fine. But things were different. There were looks and tones and feelings I no longer believed. I knew I had walked in a circle and was no farther ahead than when I set out. I was no better able to manage, I was no wiser, I had no better sense of how to go on. I could no longer pretend I hadn't been here before. I could not give myself over to the care of others. I no longer believed in their magic. My fear could not be tamed.

◦ DEPRESSION ◦

I was angry. Angry at myself for being unable to will myself to be well. Angry at all those who helped to feed the illusion that control could be had. Angry with God for breaking our deal. I had done everything he asked. I had not complained. I remember thinking of myself, "You are such a fool."

My family tolerated my ranting; they allowed me to scream at the world. I was not pleasant to be around in those days, but they did not try to placate me with sympathy or condescending remarks. They expressed their own lack of understanding. I felt like a blindfolded person whose home had been broken into. I did not know how to protect myself or my family. I could not see what I was up against. I did not know what I was fighting.

At the time, I did not know that there was an exit ramp; that there was a way to learn to get back to living a full and happy life; that I had a choice to make. All I knew was that the path I had been on had taken me in a circle. I could not see another path. I was completely and utterly lost.

I had believed that all I had to do was hang on until things got better. Now I was beginning to understand that this problem was not going to go away. I began to suffer extreme panic. Questions about life and death and the uncertain balance that holds them apart began to torment me. I struggled with the big questions: Would today be the day I would have to leave my children, my husband, my family, my life? How would my husband manage if I had another stroke? Death might be welcome to me, but what about my babies?

I began to ask questions about my relationship with God. Would God show himself? Surely I deserved to be saved. He had given me two small children for safekeeping. Did that not mean he would spare me? Thoughts of death were no longer questions that came in the dark of night. Now they were round-the-clock cries of something monstrous that refused to be silenced or controlled. I went over and over all the information I had, desperately hoping I had missed something, hoping someone could tell me how to get away from the questions that taunted me.

I was becoming aware that no one seemed able to help. I had been eating right and sleeping right and doing all the right things to stay healthy and still this had happened. I looked to my team of doctors and thought, you were the ones who said the first stroke was a fluke. Why should I believe you when you say this is never going to happen to me again? I knew they were trying to be help-ful, but I felt they were peddling false hope. They did not have the power to offer any such guarantees. Then they recommended anti-depressants to help me sleep, but the prescriptions were of no use. I had small children to care for and was damned if I was going to spend what little time I had left with them asleep.

At this point, I had a conversation with a wonderful friend, a priest. Although I had the utmost respect for his work, I cried when he told me I should pray for peace and acceptance. How could there be peace when I might have to leave my children? As for acceptance, what was it that I was supposed to accept? That this was God's will?

I had believed that I had the inner strength and resources to conquer the demon; that hard work made it possible to overcome life's circumstances; that because I was a good person, Someone or something would save me. Now it was becoming clear that it was not going to be that easy. I was beginning to understand that there are problems that cannot be fixed by out-thinking them or throwing money at them. And that being a deserving person does not grant you reprieve from suffering.

I was on hyper alert, going over and over everything. At the time, I did not realize the importance of asking questions. I simply could not keep myself from asking them: What have I got? Who can I count on? What is to become of me? What is to become of my family?

Because I did not have the answers, I hated the questions themselves. They came at me in a steady stream that could not be turned off. The medicines and the prayers that had helped silence them before did not work this time. I was too wide awake.

I especially hated it when people told me how "lucky" I was that the second stroke had not claimed more of me. Their words simply added to my torment. I did not want to believe that life depended on luck. If luck was all there was in life, then that meant I had absolutely no control and would never get off the path I was on.

I did not know that it was my anger that was helping me stay awake. I see now that being awake is the only way to ask the hard questions. At the time, I thought that asking questions about death was making me depressed. And that being depressed meant I was sick. I did not know that the questions were worthy questions. That they were profound questions that I must consider in order to learn to live differently. I thought I had fallen apart. I did not know that one must come apart in order to be put back together again.

The despair continued. I had no idea who could help me or where I could get directions. No one seemed to know what I was talking about. None of the treatments I was involved with were equipped to help me resolve the underlying fear I was feeling. I knew that somehow I must change but did not know how. All the old points of reference were gone. I no longer had confidence that I could navigate through life making choices that would keep me or my family out of harm's way.

I continued to search for someone to guide me. I sought the advice of several experts I had worked with in the field of mental health, hoping they could help me forget about death. But the prescribed relaxation treatments only served to remind me of what it felt like to die: the peace, the serenity of the moment. I would not have struggled or talked myself into coming back. I would have happily let death take me. Life-long learning had taught me to run from death. Now I knew that I could not count on myself to run. To the contrary, I might just lie there and enjoy the endless moment.

I had expected to gain some insight from all the suffering, but there was no great white light, no "aha" moment, no transport to a higher plane of insight. There was no Near-Death Experience. What lay in front of me was a blank sheet with no direction, no clues, and yet I did have an overwhelming sense that there was a great deal of work to be done.

In an effort to find some peace, I took on the task of learning about Near-Death Experiences. I suppose I was still looking for mine. What I learned was that a small percentage of people who are resuscitated from a close encounter with death report having had a series of very distinctive experiences that often significantly transformed their lives. In my mind, that put me in the non-deserving group of people waiting to be rescued only to find out that rescue may never come. Nothing I did seemed to make my life any easier.

I did not understand that death had made a permanent imprint on me and that there was no way to run from it. I did not understand what I was up against, nor did anyone else. When I tried to talk about death, it made my family very sad and caused the health-care workers to confirm their diagnosis of depression. I was afraid all the time, but I didn't know what I was afraid of.

∘ EPIPHANY OF DESPAIR ∘

Despite the fact that my health was stabilizing, I was living a life that felt foreign to me, as though I was a stranger from another country who did not speak the right dialect. On one hand, I cherished every moment I had with my children and husband: I was extremely grateful to be alive. On the other hand, I was deeply anxious and extremely lonely.

Finally one day I remembered a conversation with a patient a few years before my health crisis. While working in the department of psychiatry at the University of Alberta, I met a man who was in a great deal of distress. He had a senior job with an oil and gas company. He had a happy family life. He was someone we in health care called "highly resourced."

This man described to me how his life had been very good until he had to undergo cardiac surgery. The surgery itself had gone well, but after surgery he had developed a serious infection in his sternum and almost died. He had spent several weeks in intensive care and then several more weeks in rehabilitation. He had come to the department of psychiatry to figure out how to "get back to my old life." He asked me how he could stop himself from thinking about death. Despite the fact that his health was becoming stable, he described himself as being "off balance" and "highly anxious." He stated that he was not afraid of hard work, nor was he resistant to learning something new; he just didn't know what he was trying to learn.

I played this conversation over and over again in my mind. His statement perfectly described my life. Like him, I was prepared to do whatever needed to be done in order to regain physical function. I worked on the psychosocial scars, ready to fight to get my old life back. I was not afraid of hard work, nor was I resistant to learning something new; I just could not figure out what it was I was trying to learn. At times it gave me comfort to know that such a smart man was no more able to find his way out of the maze than I was. Other times I continued to feel totally discouraged.

Finally, as I was trying to articulate my own struggle to my husband, I heard myself ask the very same question the man had asked: What do I need to learn?

In that moment, I understood what I was asking. What did I need to learn so I could live today, tomorrow, every day that I had left, with the threat of death hanging over me?

In that moment, I began to see the true nature of what I was up against. I had been frantically looking for a way to get away from death and yet I could not stop myself from thinking about it.

In that moment, I began to understand that death is not something that goes away until one is dead. I began to think that perhaps I had been going at this backwards.

∘ ACCEPTANCE ∘

I had been thinking about death as the end point of the path of life and therefore as something I had to stay away from. I had thought death was holding me ransom, hanging over me as a threat, saying, *if you look this way, if you walk toward me, I will take you down.*

For the first time, I began to see that thinking about death did not mean I was any closer to dying. That thinking about death could perhaps help me be less afraid of dying. Perhaps death was not something to be feared but something to be listened to, something I could learn from. Perhaps the screams I heard were not death taunting me but death calling me to listen and reach out for a new way of being. I had been fighting hard to regain control of my life, but I was beginning to understand unequivocally that I could not control death. The illusion that I would ever feel in control of life had been shattered. Now I would need to learn to live differently.

I began to see that if I got over this scare, I would eventually have to deal with another, and another. We are born, we live, and we die. Even if I made it to a ripe old age and said farewell to life lying in an elegant bed, surrounded by my loved ones, I would still have to say farewell. I had been feeling like a victim and thinking of ways to protect myself. Now I was beginning to see that it was not simply my fate; it is the fate of all human beings. I was not at all alone. Death is not something any human can control. Death is part of who we are.

As strange as it may sound, this thought came to me one day as a revelation. In one single moment, I opened my eyes to the truth that we cannot deny death because it exists as part of who we are. In that moment, I realized that I had always known about death, I just had not thought about what it meant in my life. I began to understand that dying and living with the awareness that one day death will come are two very different things.

This understanding caused me a great deal of sadness but helped legitimize my pain. I began to say to myself, well, things are not perfect but you're not dead yet! I was beginning to understand the hard cold facts of life: that no matter how hard I tried, my human body would ultimately fail me. I did not have control over my body's breaking down, whether it happened through illness, trauma, or old age. I was going to die and no one could save me. And I could not save myself.

It was as though a little pathway in the forest opened up and for the first time I could see that there might be another way to think about things. I could see I had a choice to make: Am I going to be afraid and sit here waiting for death to take me? Or, am I going to recognize the fear and yet commit to search for a way to live with death?

In one way, it was so depressing. But in another, it was almost funny, because I started to say to myself, what the hell was I thinking — of course I'm going to die one day. Of course I'm not happy about it. Of course no one else wants to talk about it. It *is* depressing.

Whatever problems I had, I began to weigh them against being dead.

The struggles I had gone through began to make sense. I began to be able to articulate my concerns in a way that others could understand. I began to see that along with the loss of innocence I had in fact gained some insight. Now, rather than being more afraid, I was becoming less afraid. I did not have power to prevent dying, but I did have a choice about how I dealt with the knowledge of death. I began to think about dying and death as two separate things. Dying would come one day no matter what, but how I chose to live knowing it would come one day was something else. Nothing was harder than to deal head on with death. Yet nothing gave me as great an opportunity to feel stronger.

I still had feelings of regret for what I no longer had, but I no longer thought in terms of whose fault it was. It was just life. It was the reality of the world, of the human frailty we all share. Over the months and years, I had come to terms with the fact that I had both physical and mental limitations. I had a clear understanding that there had been a change in my situation. But only when I started to understand that it was death that I was raging against did I learn to stop trying to control things. I stopped looking for a reason. I stopped trying to get answers to unanswerable questions.

I had been angry with God for not coming in the way I thought he should. Now I was beginning to rethink that. I was still conflicted about God's lack of presence in my hour of need. But I could see that he had never claimed he would prevent death. I was beginning to understand that I must somehow bridge Life and Death. I must create a place in my life for both. I would become a student and learn to live with death. I would prepare myself for death, but I would continue to live while alive.

◦ ACQUIRING RESOURCES — SELF, OTHERS, GOD ◦

At the time, I had not developed the language I needed to put into words what I was feeling. So I took a pragmatic approach. A major reason that death had so much power over me was my concern for the well being of my children. I began to organize them so they would not be harmed if I had to leave. I took individual pictures of each of them with each and every family member. I hung the whole series of pictures on their bedroom wall. Every morning and every night I asked them in turn, "Who loves you the most in the whole world?" Then we would go through saying each family member's name as we pointed them out. In the event that I had to go, the children must be safe. The only way I could ensure their safety was to make sure they had an abundance of people who loved them. I knew their daddy would do his best, but we were in love and he would be sad.

I had it in my mind that the best way to keep my children safe was to stop being the hub of the family wheel and just be a spoke. A wheel can keep operating if one spoke is bent or removed.

I felt that each and every family member must have their own relationship with my children independent of me. I talked to our families about how much responsibility might lie ahead in the event of my departure. They were not comfortable with what I was saying, but they began to grasp my rationale. I told them that if I had to leave, I did not want my children's lives ruined. The more involved with them they were now, the more "life insurance" my children would have if the need arose. It was tough to think in those terms but it was necessary, given what we were up against. The outcome of this way of thinking has been very positive: my children have formed profound attachments to the members of our larger family.

Once I could reconcile how to prepare my children for a life without me, I went out in search of support for myself. I began to seek out the real experts on the topic of death: those who had suffered trauma in their lives. I spoke to mothers and fathers who had lost children and to children who had lost parents. I spoke to those who were living with a terminal diagnosis, as well as to many who had survived an experience of almost dying. There was always one question, spoken or unspoken, that they asked me before they shared: "Are you sincere in your quest to know?" My own health crisis seemed to allow me entrance to a secret club. My ability to share my own health challenges became my personal competitive advantage.

There appeared to be two groups in this club. Some spoke with a great deal of sorrow about the life they once had and with a yearning for the old life they would never return to. These people seemed to be stuck in a life they were not fully connected to. They were still running from death, on the circular path I knew all too well. They seemed to be paralyzed by fear, waiting for their miracle. While I could relate to their pain, I desperately did not want to remain part of their group.

In the other group were those who were able to share stories of wisdom and gratitude, people who were living full lives despite the trauma they had suffered. They were pragmatic and strategic. I wanted to be like them. There were many things to be learned. They became my guides.

I began to think more strategically about how I would learn to live again. I could see from these people that I had been consumed by the fear of dying, and that, as a result, I was not truly open to experiencing life.

I began to think that I couldn't go on being this scared, always being ready to leave. So I started taking as good care of myself as I could. If I was going to have to leave my children, it was not going to be my fault. I went to the gym every day, trying to get myself into the best shape I could. With that, I began to learn how to trust myself physically. Not trust that my body would never break down again, but trust that I could find the balance between pushing myself and learning what my limitations were.

At first I was so afraid to push myself at all; then I went the other way and beat myself up when my body would not produce the way it used to. Slowly I learned not to overreact when I felt weak and not to let myself off the hook.

I realized that I was holding myself back from the people I loved. I was afraid to love too much. I had to develop the courage not to distance myself from loved ones just because I knew how it would end.

I also had to learn how to be more honest with people. That was a hard one. I had to learn to declare to people that I needed help. Some people were not that kind. So I had to work at surrounding myself with the people I wanted to have around me, while seeing that I needed to forgive others for not understanding. I had to learn to become gentler with those who might not know the truths about life and death. In seeing it that way, I began to accept others' limitations. The outcome for me was a sense of freedom to have open relationships with people, forgiving them for not being more than they are. I learned to embrace life and the goodness of people. I realize now that to give help and accept help are both great privileges. It is in the giving as well as the receiving that we become part of something beyond ourselves. Many of us do the one far better than the other.

For a long time I was afraid to compete. I would begin to challenge myself and then run home the moment I received any criticism. I felt I had to prove something to others. Ultimately I found that the more experience I had, the better able I was to accept criticism and take direction. The more open I was, the more feedback people were willing to give me and the better informed I would become.

A year after my second stroke, I decided to study recovery in a more formal way. At the time, school seemed a safe way to challenge myself, since the consequence of failing would affect only me. In 1994 I began studying for a master's degree in the department of Adult Education and Counselling Psychology at the University of Toronto. Getting through the coursework was quite a production. My sister, my husband, and my children all took turns transcribing the lectures I taped. There were many tears and many long walks to school when I wondered what the heck I was doing. In hindsight, I see that it was a very ambitious undertaking but a safe alternative to grinding it out in the work world or hiding away at my home. As humbling as it was to have to do everything longhand, the process of studying reminded me of how great it felt to learn again. And knowing that I could learn, however differently, made me want to go on.

While completing that degree, I conducted a major research project, *Recovery as Perceived by the Client*. I interviewed people who had suffered from different physical traumas (car accident, cancer, gunshot wound, stroke, and spinal cord injury). I was interested in the research that would document the experience of recovery in a pragmatic way: research that did not focus on the cause of trauma but rather on the process of recovery.

The people I interviewed were generous in sharing their insights in considerable detail. Several commented that they had been asked to tell their story many times but no one had ever asked them for "the whole story." All claimed to be extremely grateful to family and friends. All invariably stated that they had received excellent health care. It was interesting, then, to hear one after the other state that despite these great resources, they had felt alone. That they had wanted to talk about what they knew, but their loved ones had found it too hard to listen.

Each one spoke about the struggles they had endured while making sense of death. They stated that awareness of death had caused a great deal of distress but that their recovery had depended on learning to live with death. These people were describing a specific path to recovery. They all claimed that learning about death had enhanced their living. For the first time, I could see that we who had suffered might know more about life, not less.

My interactions with these kind people taught me a great deal. I realized that I had developed insights from a greater knowledge of death. Death had become part of my everyday life. I was using death as a reminder to be grateful for life. It was this awareness that made me delighted to open my eyes every morning. It was death that made me grateful to have another day with those I loved.

I began to wonder if it was possible to map the learning of the people I was studying to benefit those who were still searching. More research was necessary to describe the process of learning to live with death.

After receiving my master's degree, I spent a year interviewing dozens of academics and professionals before I found the program best suited my needs. In 2000 I began a Ph.D. in the department of theology at the University of Wales. I had studied the physical aspects of dying, as well as the psycho-social aspects of recovery; now I felt that looking at the psychospiritual aspects of death might help me to develop yet another vantage point.

My doctoral dissertation was an interdisciplinary piece of research into how the topic of death is understood and dealt with in our health-conscious, age-defying Western society (Hatanaka, 2005: *From Death to Life: The Process of Learning to Live with the Knowledge That Death Is Real*). It showed how those who had learned to live with death were able to articulate the important role that death played in their recovery. They described themselves as members of an exclusive club, one that all will eventually join. Doing a Ph.D. degree is an extremely arduous process for someone who has had a head injury, but no harder than gathering up the nerve to venture out of my house again after the day I got lost. The people I have interviewed and the ones I now see in my private practice brave extraordinary obstacles every day. In the chapters that follow, stories about five of them will guide you through the process of learning to live.

I have learned a great deal from the hundreds of people who have shared their wisdom with me. I know how hard it is to find one's way. I know that the burden of the search can be so heavy at times that one can be crushed under its weight. I know that the friends who are of most value are the ones who show compassion. They are not always the ones with the most time, but they are the ones who will respond when called upon. They are the ones who understand reciprocity and the importance of being trusted. Interestingly, they are often the ones who have suffered themselves.

There is a certain look on the faces of people who have been humbled by life. We who have suffered carry ourselves differently. It is hard work being fully engaged in life while knowing we must be prepared to leave. It takes a lot of energy to make sure the slate is clean so we don't leave any messes for others to clean up when we are gone. It sounds simple, but it remains the hardest thing we do. In some ways, we are very fragile, at the mercy of death. But in another way, we are fearless, knowing we are out in front of the learning that awaits every person. We cannot be threatened or tormented in the same way.

I remember sitting at a large table at the University of Wales surrounded by brilliant and serious scholars about to hear my doctoral defense. It was one of those cold wet UK days, and inside, things were no less dark and dreary. But I smiled to myself and thought, I am ready to begin. After all, how serious can this be? Are they going to kill me?

Indeed, I have come to think about the world differently. As a mother who has learned that death is real, I can no longer look at my children and say, "Love only me." I look at them and say to them, "Love me and be open to love in your life. Allow others to love you so you will be safe with or without me."

In teaching my children how to be loved by others, I in turn have become open to the concept of loving other women's children, the bereaved children of parents who have not been able to stay and love them.

In 2001, we adopted twin girls. They came to us as souls in need of care, but they brought with them a bond that connects all people of the world. Through our interaction with them, we have all become witnesses to the great love that the human heart is capable of.

It is wisdom that replaces the innocence lost.

INTERGENERATIONAL GRIEF

Michael's story

In death, a family may band together, learn to suffer together, and eventually acquire the resources necessary to cope with the loss. Or a family may become divided, with some members developing strategies to cope and others not.

Suffering places a terrible burden of hardship on a person and a family, but suffering in and of itself does not damage the soul of a person. By no means am I saying that people ought to suffer or that I wish them to suffer. I am saying that we are hard-wired for suffering. It is part of being human, and we've been doing it since the beginning of time. However, if one does not "suffer well" — that is, if one is not supported and cared for, if one does not experience relief from suffering — then the weight of the suffering can turn into something else: anger, resentment, and bitterness. In order to survive in such a family, one may need to become somewhat detached. With a lack of attachment to each other, the problems deepen *and spread over the years and across the generations, introducing a whole series of other unpleasant habits and behaviors that can seriously weaken a family.*

We all know of families who exhibit the effects of such damage: families who do not show kindness to each other, who antagonize each other, who do not communicate. Perhaps you come from such a family yourself: one of your parents' siblings may have died; your grandmother may have been widowed; or your family may have escaped from a war-torn country. Grief can transcend generations, sending families into a vicious cycle of suffering. The Grief Reconciliation Process can help people break out of the negative cycle of grief and start building a healthier foundation for the future.

The problem described by the story of a man named Michael is unfortunately all too common. The help he received is, in the same way, also all too rare.

Michael and Jenna were a loving young married couple. They had met at Boston University when they were both doing their MBAs. It was love at first sight. At least that's how Jenna described it. She loved the way Michael moved. She loved the way he smelled. She loved how singularly focused he was. She loved how smart he made her feel. She loved how strong he was: when he took her in his arms, she felt completely safe. Michael would laugh and say he'd finally found someone who could keep up with him. Both were enjoying successful careers and together they had formed many friendships within their community.

They had been married for two and a half years when at dinner one night Jenna brought up the topic of children. Michael was quick to remind her of their decision not to discuss children until they were settled into their own home. It would be several years before they were able to take on the financial responsibility of children. Jenna acknowledged the conversation they'd had, but wanted to tell him about her friend's new baby girl. She wanted to share with him how she felt when she helped her friend, and how anxious she was to have her own — his — baby. In the middle of the conversation, Michael got up walked out of the room.

It wasn't the first time Jenna had seen him shut down when he didn't want to discuss something. He had done it several times before. They had talked about the way he ended such discussions and tried to resolve it, but anytime Jenna was upset, he would tell her in many different ways to stop, just stop, being upset. And that if she couldn't stop being upset, then she should have the good sense to shut up.

As much as she loved him, Jenna hated this about him. In fact, it made her angry, very angry, and this particular time she told him so.

"Stop walking away from me when I'm trying to tell you how I feel," she yelled.

He mumbled something that she clearly was not meant to hear and kept right on walking.

Jenna followed him, accusing him of not trusting her enough to want to explain his position. Of not loving her enough to share what was really going on.

She hoped he would take offense, would bark something at her the way her sister used to do when they fought. Then they could have a real discussion. She hoped he would tell her that she had it wrong, that he loved her and needed her to understand what he was going through. Instead, she got nothing more than a hauntingly distant look: a blank stare that said I don't really care what you think.

Jenna cried herself to sleep that night. He did not come to her. By morning, she was physically and emotionally exhausted. She dragged herself out of bed and walked down to the kitchen, half expecting to find Michael slumped over, asleep on the couch. Instead, she found him dressed, replete with shirt and tie, getting ready to walk out the door. He looked shockingly unaffected by what had happened the night before.

Michael was late coming home from work the following night. Late enough for Jenna to begin to wonder if he had met someone new. Was he having an affair? How much did he expect her to put up with? Again she cried herself to sleep.

By the next morning, Jenna was back to being angry: with herself for being so pathetically weak and vulnerable, and with Michael for being such a self-centered ass. She decided to go on the offensive. She got herself dressed for work, rehearsed what she wanted to say, and then went down to the kitchen to deliver her speech. Michael was sitting at the counter, reading the newspaper. He scarcely looked up.

Jenna started by explaining to him that she wanted to know that they could discuss anything. When Michael did not respond, she went on, "But that is not true for you, is it? You think it's perfectly fine to distance yourself whenever you feel like it."

She waited for him to reply. When he did not, she said, "When you act this way, you make me want to shut down, too. You make me want to get away from you."

With Michael still not responding, her anger got the best of her. "I can't take this anymore," she said. "I'm going home for a while."

She went to their bedroom and packed a small bag. Michael sat at the counter and made no attempt to follow her. When she came back into the kitchen, she was no longer angry. Her eyes were filled with tears. She stared at him, silently pleading with him to make her reconsider her departure, to say something, anything.

Finally, she broke through the silence with, "Honey, I love you, but there is something very wrong and we need to sort out what it is. I want to know about you. I want to know who you really are, and how you think and what you want. I want you to wake up and get involved with me, too. I don't want to be pushed away from the man I love. I've said a million times that we should get some help with this, but clearly you don't want to work on it together. So I am going to get some help for myself and I want you to go and get some help, too. You should go see a psychiatrist."

She reached past him, hoping he would take her hand, and lifted her keys off the counter. Then she walked out the door.

Michael sat there alone, not knowing what came next. It had never occurred to him that she would actually leave.

Over the next few days, he tried not to think about Jenna. He tried to convince himself that he didn't care. He worked long hours and played squash with his friends. But he could not get away from her. The image of her was with him all day long. The scent of her was on his clothes. He missed coming home to her smile and warm embrace. He missed calling her in the middle of the day. He missed having her in his bed.

He was so sure she would just cool off and come home that he did nothing for the first few days besides miss her.

By the third day, Michael began to think more strategically about what it might take to solve the problem. The weight of her words began to sink in. If seeing a psychiatrist was what it would take to make her happy, then perhaps he could do that.

With no appreciation for what he might learn about himself, Michael walked into the office of a psychiatrist whose office he passed on his way home from work every night. There he met Dr. Fergusson Dalziel, who approached him with an engaging smile and a warm handshake. A few minutes later, Dr. Dalziel's assistant had confirmed initial bookings at Michael's request for three times a week for the next two weeks. Michael intended to get the whole thing over with as quickly as possible.

The first get-together was the following afternoon at precisely 3 p.m. The pattern of the appointment repeated itself at subsequent sessions that week: a slow start followed by a heightened intensity as the two men explored the universe of emotional possibilities.

By the end of the second week, a pattern was becoming more apparent to the psychiatrist: the more innocuous the question, the more expansive Michael's response; the more intrusive the question, the more Michael would shut down. Dr. Dalziel had observed this behavior in children who had suffered loss or trauma: children of war victims and children whose experience in foster homes had been fraught with formality or lack of intimacy.

Michael's initial hesitancy slowly turned into curiosity about where the good doctor's line of questioning would lead them.

He was also becoming more attuned to Dr. Dalziel's style of questioning: how he often paraphrased the words he used to end a thought, making them the core of the next question posed. For example, Michael would say, "That is so typical of my wife," and the psychiatrist would say, "Typical? In what way?" and off they would go.

Over time, Michael began to enjoy his dialogues with Dr. Dalziel. The discussions were quite unlike what he had anticipated. Instead of pouring out his heart to a passive observer, he found himself intrigued by this intelligent individual who kept asking about prior feelings versus future plans.

Indeed, the doctor was looking for the appropriate moment to articulate his initial thoughts to Michael.

The moment came when Michael was on a rant about there being no past, just a present and a future, to which Dr. Dalziel responded, "You see me as a psychiatrist, when in fact I am two things: I am a psychiatrist and a historian. In your situation, I believe both are relevant. If we are to get your wife to really know you and understand you, it is critical that you get to know and understand yourself first."

Michael's sigh showed Dr. Dalziel that he wasn't really following his line of thought, so he said, "Let me lay it out for you, Michael. Your paradigm, or the way you view the world, is greatly influenced by the circumstances in which you grew up. Everything you did or saw or heard as a child, all of the events and happenings within your family, have profoundly influenced your sense of who you are today as you sit here in front of me. Therefore, it is not just important, it is critical to have a sense of how things were for prior generations as well. Just like the remnants of previous civilizations, they provide the foundational cornerstones upon which each successive generation is built.

"The strength, the resilience, and the insights of generations past, or the lack thereof, play a powerful role in determining the way the current generation interacts with the world. For example, the chains of grief and trauma can go back three or four generations.

"The logical extension of this foundational reality is that your individual responses are often learned by modeling the actions of the previous generation. Therefore my initial advice to you is to step back and reach into the past, to pursue knowledge and context that will help you to understand your instinctive responses to various situations. The key to your enlightened decision-making is to absorb as much learning from the past as you can so that you can begin to develop self-knowledge.

"Anyway, sorry to get technical on you, but what I mean to say is that you should go visit your parents and your grandparents. There should be no question in your mind that this is going to be a lot of work, so my question to you, Michael, is, 'How hard are you willing to work?' "

At the time, Michael didn't know what any of this meant to him or to his relationship with his wife. But he was curious and agreed to the assignment.

"Perhaps you could begin by asking your parents about their parents," Dr. Dalziel said. "Ask them to tell you about your grandparents. The reaction you get from the question will give you clues about your family history. Either they will encourage you to learn about your ancestors, their trials, their burdens, their joys. Or they may say it is too difficult to talk about this. They may tell you they don't want to go back, or they may simply avoid answering you altogether."

Michael was back to saying nothing, so Dr. Dalziel continued, "Think about your grandparents' lives as the walls of the foundation upon which you are built. There are four walls: paternal grandfather, paternal grandmother, maternal grandfather, and maternal grandmother. Go find out what the walls are made of and get as much information on each grandparent as you can."

Michael began his project by going home to visit his parents. He began with his dad, who was delighted to share what he knew about his parents. He even went one step further and suggested that Michael might enjoy visiting them. Within a few hours, he had made arrangements for Michael to do just that on the coming weekend. Michael was starting to see what Dr. Dalziel meant about the access to information. It appeared it was going to be easy to access his father's family history.

Michael's visit with his paternal grandparents was different from visits in the past. For the first time, he wanted to know about them, not as grandparents but as a husband and wife facing various challenges, as man and woman in the world they grew up in. He listened hard in order to learn more about himself. He asked about their hardships. He sat for hours as they told him their many stories, some tragic, others triumphant, all ending with the clear message that the family must suffer and rejoice together.

A few days later, Michael went home again, but this time to speak to his mother. As he began to talk to her, she appeared uncomfortable. When Michael pushed her a bit, she said she was prepared to discuss her father's family, with whom she had a warm relationship. She took out pictures of her father's home and talked about visits to his parents' home when she was a child.

She went on to say that her dad would be "a different man had he not been burdened with a sick wife." She described her father as a quiet man who deserved a lot of sympathy. He was the one in charge of keeping her crazy mother from creating too much chaos. When it came time to talk about her mother, she was unwilling to discuss that side of the family at all.

Michael realized that he knew very little about his maternal grandmother other than that she had caused a lot of trouble for his mom. When he was in elementary school, she would call his mom in the middle of the night. She had trouble with drugs and alcohol. He and his siblings had been taught as young children never to trust her. She was tolerated but not welcome in their home. Everyone accepted that it was best not to count on her. His grandfather would try to keep the peace whenever things started getting out of hand. Together, they were just there in the background of Michael's life. He didn't expect anything from them, and they never delivered. For the first time, Michael was curious to know more about that. He booked another several weeks of sessions with Dr. Dalziel.

As another week passed, Michael added little pieces to the blueprint of his "foundation." Three of the walls were looking relatively intact despite some scars; it was this fourth one he still knew little about. Michael dropped in on his parents several more times to find out more about his mother's parents, but it continued to be hard for him to get anything out of her. Finally his mother asked him outright to steer clear of the topic. At the next session, he explained to Dr. Dalziel how annoyed he was with his mother for keeping family information from him.

The doctor asked, "What if something has happened to make your mother feel like she needs to protect herself from her own mother? What if it is pain that she does not want to share with you? What if she feels like she needs to protect you?"

Michael had never thought about that. He had always thought of his mother as being tough, focused, and fearless. In fact, she could be quite rigid and controlling. It was hard for him to imagine her being afraid of anything.

Dr. Dalziel said, "Well, sometimes people develop thick outer coats to protect themselves. They learn to wrap themselves in layers and detach themselves so they won't get hurt anymore. If this is true, what happened? So now we come to the decision: Are you willing to dig deep — to really understand what went on with your family — or does the trail end here with stories untold and nothing really reconciled?"

Those words stuck with Michael. Jenna's words and the doctor's began to blend together: "Do you want to get involved? Do you want to know yourself? Or do you want to just go on in life without getting involved in any issues?"

He walked home with Jenna's voice whispering to him, "I want you to wake up and get involved."

When Michael got home, he phoned his maternal grandparents. His grandfather was out and his grandmother responded as she always did: with an explanation for why today might not be the best day. Before she got any further, Michael announced that he was coming over.

His grandmother received him with a warm hello, followed by excuses for why she looked a mess; why the house was not as tidy as it should be; why she hadn't been over to see them. She gave him a loose hug and then didn't seem to know what to do with him.

Michael watched for a way to ease into the conversation. He tried to sit next to her, but she fussed with the cushions and then moved away. Without the perfect moment presenting itself, he said, "Grandma, I've realized lately that I don't know much about when you were a little girl."

She was quiet for a moment and then said, "I don't think there's much to tell."

"Let's start with where you lived."

After another moment, she answered, "Well, first I lived with my parents and then after my mom died I lived with a whole bunch of people."

"How old were you when your mom died?"

"Oh, I don't know, maybe seven or ten or something like that."

Michael was shocked that she didn't know. "What happened to your mom?"

"I don't really know. It was a long time ago." She got up and poured herself an "afternoon cocktail."

Case closed.

When his grandfather got home, he acknowledged how nice it was to have Michael there but made no attempt to offer anything more by way of conversation. His grandparents did not speak to each other. She sipped her drink. He picked up the newspaper and settled into his chair.

Michael was beginning to understand the life his mother must have lived. Did she get that kind of reaction when she came home from school? Did she walk into a home filled with such apathy? Was she forced to watch her mother drown her sorrows every day? It was no wonder his mother could be distant and cold. No wonder she was so preoccupied with her own success. No wonder she lacked the ability to greet him with any kind of warmth when he came home. She had never had that herself. For the first time, he understood how lonely his mother must have been. How difficult her life was.

Michael was beginning to feel some discomfort over his research assignment. He was worried about pushing his mother. He did not want to force her to remember days that had caused her a lot of pain. He was glad when he was able to see Dr. Dalziel again.

"Are there any other family members who could help you get the information you need?" Dr. Dalziel asked.

Michael thought long and hard on that one. He thought about asking his mother's sisters, but his mother had very little connection to them. He settled instead on his grandmother's oldest sister, Joan, who had been very kind to his mom over the years. Maybe she could tell him about his great-grandmother's death. So he drove over to visit her.

Joan was not at all like his grandmother. She had survived the death of her husband and successfully raised her children on her own. She greeted Michael with a warm smile and a strong hug. Michael explained to her that he was trying to find out more about his grandmother, her little sister.

She was quite willing to accommodate his request. She poured them both some tea and then came to sit next to him on the couch. She explained how the death of their mother had set off a chain of events that had made life difficult for everyone. At the time they all did whatever they could to survive. As she told the family story, Michael began to see things very differently. A new version of his grandmother's life assembled itself in his mind's eye.

He saw Joan's little sister, Clara, as an eight-year-old girl playing with her toys, going to school, learning to read, being tucked in at night by her mother. Then one morning Clara gets out of bed and wanders down to the kitchen. She finds her father bent over at the kitchen table, tears streaming down his face. Her middle sister and older brother are standing on either side, trying to console him.

Clara doesn't dare ask what is wrong. Instead, she goes to find her mother. She searches in the living room. There are a couple of people huddled together on the couch. She doesn't recognize them. She goes outside to the veranda. She finds a friend of her father's sitting in silence. He does not welcome her.

Quickly, little Clara turns and runs up the stairs. She makes her way to her mother's bedroom. She can hear voices and opens the door expecting to find her mother and her aunt sharing secrets. Instead, she finds her aunt and her eldest sister standing over her mother with a washcloth. Clara stands there expecting her mother to call for her. She doesn't. The women turn to Clara, tears in their eyes. They do not welcome her. Instead, they turn and continue to wash.

The little girl listens for the voice of her mother. She stands perfectly still, waiting, hoping. She backs up and leans against the wall. Still her mother has not moved. Slowly she approaches the bed. Her aunt turns to her and says, "Off you go, child. This is no place for you."

Clara sits alone at the top of the stairs. Over the next few hours, she pieces the story together. Her mother has died. The baby her mother was carrying has died. Clara would not be a big sister, and she would no longer be a child. Everything is awful, and the only thing she can do to help is to be good and keep quiet.

For the next several months, the grief in the house is so thick, it is hard to breathe; everyone is consumed by it. The boys take over the father's chores on the farm. The older girls take over the mother's many jobs. Little Clara is assigned the task of behaving. The best way for her to help is to not make more work for the others. She learns not to ask for much, not to take much. She does not argue when, in his deep grief, her father sends her to live with various neighbors. Clara retreats into her own little world of surviving.

Michael left his great-aunt's home full of thought. He did not know how to feel about what he had been told.

Later that week, he talked to Dr. Dalziel about his break-through visit.

"Let's consider for a moment what you've learned about your family," Dr. Dalziel said. "Let's think about grandma and how she learned to survive. Perhaps she is still trying to survive today. She gets up every morning and tries, in whatever way she can, to make it through the day. The pattern of surviving has become so ingrained in who she is that she has never learned anything else. When she was little, she did what she could to accommodate her family. But instead of living with people who would help her to digest the reality of death that she was faced with, she lived with people who wanted her to forget, people who wanted her to be quiet and good.

"When little Clara began to assess that things were different and life was going to be hard without her mother, she was sent off to live with various people, none of whom was able to relate directly to her pain. Instead of learning how to move ahead in life, how to learn to live with the cards she had been dealt, she had to learn to numb herself or the pain of her situation would overwhelm her. She learned that the best way to be numb was to be half asleep.

"When she was little, she could retreat into a fantasy world in order to survive, but as she got older perhaps it became harder for her to ignore the pain. Perhaps as she got older, she learned how to self-medicate in order to take the edge off and get through the day. As she grew older, she began using alcohol and drugs as tools to keep herself asleep.

"The problem if you go to sleep when you are little is that it gets harder and harder to wake up. Perhaps as she grew up the pattern of survival has become so ingrained in her that she simply never acquired any skills to learn to live. Perhaps she has always been afraid of what it might mean to be awake. To her being awake may mean being in pain. There had been no one to help her with the pain, so unknowingly she decided that she might have to stay asleep.

"So, perhaps your grandma went around and around in a never-ending cycle of grief, never learning to reconcile the death of her mother. All she ever learned was to numb the pain and try to forget. When she grew up, she married into the same type of relationship that she saw modeled in her family: her husband was a caretaker type who helped her avoid the truth. She had three children because that is what she was supposed to do. She raised them but with much difficulty. She spent most of her life depressed, unable to take on any circumstance that was unpleasant, including that of her daughter who was demanding. She did not develop a language to articulate her fears of being alone or her grief. She did not learn to live with death. Her response to all stress was to retreat to becoming a patient: take a Valium along with a glass of wine and go to bed.

"While your grandmother is the one who experienced the death first-hand, your mother has been greatly impacted by your grandmother's grief. Perhaps she has inherited the behaviors of a survivor: do what you must to get by; do not get too engaged. Stay neutral; stay partly asleep so you can conserve your energy."

Michael asked the doctor why his mother didn't seem to know.

"Close family members may well know about the tragedy, but as time passes, the death and the suffering may be forgotten while the destructive behaviors live on. Children may simply know their parent as someone who is pathetic and drinks too much, or is distant and cold. Seldom is one taught how to go in search of the reason or what to do about it. They do not know about living with death.

"So the children learn to detach themselves from the problem in order to survive themselves. If you are detached from your family, then there is no support system in place to help you with anything. You look around and think to yourself, there is only me. I had better take control here. So you start to control all the things you can and you detach yourself from anything you can't control. Like sometimes people.

"Maybe your mom grew up feeling totally alone because she could not count on her mother, and her father was too busy 'looking after mother.' Maybe the only way she could resolve those feelings was to detach herself and she began to feel nothing but disgust for this woman who constantly made it clear that she would not be around to help. From what you've told me, your mother went on to strive to be anything other than her mother. In doing so, she became externally focused and craved praise for her success. Perhaps that is why she openly calls her mother pathetic and professes that she had been dealt a terrible set of cards in being born to such a weak woman.

"But what if your mother, like her mother, did not know how to help those she loved to develop emotionally? She too suffered from attachment issues. Raised by a mother who had a grief-induced attachment disorder, she was distant. Rather than teach her children that they could count on her both in good times and bad, her goal was simply to keep everyone from being 'unhappy.' Either shut them up or fix them. When emotions bubbled up and got too much for her, she simply avoided the person."

Michael could not remember his mother ever discussing anything of any significance with him, nor could he remember sharing any deep joy with her. Even as a young boy, she had never been able or willing to show him tenderness. She simply took care of the basics. He could not remember his parents ever hugging each other or laughing together.

"My parents did not physically leave each other, but they didn't rely on each other, either," he said. "They both quietly went about doing their own thing. They never really argued or showed passion to each other. They were more like roommates."

Michael was beginning to see that like both his grandmother and his mother, he might not have developed the ability to engage in helping out when there was suffering. He simply tried to get away from the source of the pain. He was beginning to feel a great deal of sadness for his grandmother, his mother, his father — the entire family. They had been greatly affected by death, and yet none of them except his great-aunt seemed to have developed any skills to deal with it.

The doctor was glad for Michael's involvement in understanding his family. "And now, with you, Michael," he said, "we have this great guy who does not really want to just survive. You want to love your wife and have her back. You do not really want to settle for avoiding the issues like they did. If you did, you wouldn't be here. You wouldn't have fallen in love with someone who was going to push you to stay awake. You would have married someone different."

Michael began to see that the trouble between him and his wife was symptomatic. Like his mother, he had developed strategies to survive in life, to try to make do. When the going got a little rough, he was well rehearsed in detaching himself from the source of pain.

He was beginning to see that neither he nor his family was the root cause of the problem. All were simply reacting in different ways to suffering that had begun long ago with the death of a loved one. For the first time, he wanted to wake up. He did not want to cover up pain; he wanted to expose it in order to understand its significance.

The doctor explained to Michael that there would be many months — years — of hard work ahead for him. But Michael was not deterred. For the first time a blueprint had become evident. He was determined to learn to assess his situation and learn to acquire the skills he would need to build a strong foundation.

Michael left the doctor's office that day more awake than ever before. He was not angry; he was sad. Sad that he hadn't known about all of this before. Sad for his parents. Sad to think that he had inadvertently settled for being a survivor and that it might be too late for Jenna and him.

He made his way to Jenna's parents' home. He stood on the front step, alone, afraid to ring the bell. Afraid to face what waited for him on the other side of the door. He thought about turning away, but he could not: if he did, he would be going back to the old way of handling things. He did not want that. He slowly put his hand up and rang the bell.

When Jenna answered the door, Michael said, "I want to talk."

Jenna wrapped her arms around his neck and began to cry. "I've been waiting to hear those words for many years," she said.

Michael took her into his arms while she cried, and said, "Let's go home."

STRIVING TO BE WHOLE

Jim's Story

In the interviews I have conducted there is always one inescapable reality. The physiological and psychological factors are only part of the process of recovery. In order to recover fully, we must commit ourselves to the arduous negotiation process of learning to live with death.

This negotiation process results in the deals we strike with ourselves to keep fighting to live; those we must strike with others, who may or may not know how to be supportive; and the spiritual conflict as we try to answer the big question: "How do I go on, now that I know that death lives at the core of who I am?"

In this story, we see the extreme challenges met by one who journeyed from being a highly confident young man to almost dying, and back to living a full life.

It describes a young man who survived a devastating physical trauma only to find out that surviving was just the beginning of *his journey. He was prepared to work hard to overcome the physical and psychological setbacks of this trauma, but what he did not understand for many months was that to fully recover he would have to learn to live with death.*

In his struggles to survive, he reconciled his physical limitations. In allowing himself to be loved by others, he gained knowledge of his psychological confines. In learning to live with death, he met his soul.

It was a beautiful spring day. The air was fresh after the previous night's rain. Jim was crossing the university football field, on his way back to his dorm after toiling through a vicious chemistry lesson, when he heard a familiar voice call his name. He turned, saw a couple of his friends tossing a football around, and then heard someone yell, "Heads up, Jim." Instinctively, he threw his knapsack down, jumped high in the air, and focused on catching the football hurtling toward him. He made a catch that earned him cheers from several students nearby, but as he tried to find his footing, he slipped on the wet grass and fell in an awkward heap.

That was the last moment Jim would remember of his old life. He felt himself fall to the ground in what seemed like slow motion. Without his usual athletic grace, he hit the ground head first, rolling onto his back. He lay there for a moment and found himself looking up at the bluest sky he had ever seen. He felt a serenity he had never experienced before. He was irritated by the sound of people calling his name. They were calling him back from a state of perfect rest. Then his friends came into focus: they were huddled over him, at first laughing nervously, hoping he was joking, then expressing their concern in gasps and screams, which Jim realized he could hear but not respond to.

A wave of panic washed over him. He closed his eyes and then opened them, trying hard to hit the reset button. Then he closed them again.

∘ Surviving ∘

The next time Jim opened his eyes, he was lying in a bed. He scanned the room, searching for clues. Nothing was familiar: not the lighting, not the pictures on the wall, not the sounds, not the smells. He lay there trying to remember what lapse of judgment had landed him in this place. Then he tried to move. Excruciating pain attacked him from all sides: his head was pounding; his left arm was tied down to accommodate needles that ran into his veins; he could not move his legs.

While he was still trying to orient himself, two strangers entered the room and mumbled something to him about needing to go somewhere. Before he had a chance to process what they were saying, the strangers pulled the covers off him. The cold air ran up his back. Without waiting for him to try to salvage his dignity, they pulled him off his bed, lifted his partially clad body onto a gurney, and wheeled him out of the room. Jim struggled to pull the sheet up as they made their way out the door.

The air in the hallway was cold and noise was coming at him

from all directions. People stared at him as he was wheeled into the elevator. They had odd looks on their faces. Jim couldn't tell whether they were embarrassed at having invaded his personal space or annoyed because he had invaded theirs. He decided to close his eyes and pretend not to see them.

When the stretcher stopped, Jim was shifted again, this time onto a cold table around which more strangers huddled. They spoke a series of words he didn't understand — spinal cord injury; limited mobility; lack of sensitivity in lower limbs — but in a tone of voice that made him realize he was in trouble. His body was pulled and pushed and touched in ways he had never experienced. He was told to lie there and endure the torture. Jim used every ounce of energy he had not to cry. He had no real understanding of what they were saying. The doctors spoke among themselves, reviewing the last several weeks of treatment.

When Jim was finally taken back to his room, he found his father waiting for him. Jim let out the breath he had been holding, and tears began to stream down his face. "Things aren't that bad," he whispered to his father. It was a statement, not a question. He was hoping not to be corrected. Saying nothing, his father put his hand under Jim's legs and helped the attendant lift him back into bed. Jim noticed the strain the weight of his legs put on his father. He tried to help but realized again that his legs would not respond.

Panic shot through him. "How bad is it?" he asked.

His dad leaned over and kissed his forehead.

It had been a long time since Jim had felt his dad's kiss. It reminded him of his parents' nightly rituals when he was a kid, which had succeeded in keeping the night terrors away. He grabbed onto that memory. The terror that was beginning to overwhelm him was offset by the strength of his father's touch. At least for the moment, it was easier not to ask any more questions.

His body was throbbing and he still had no understanding of where he was or why, but somehow having his father there meant he didn't have to worry about everything right now. On a visceral level, he knew he was in trouble, but he didn't have the energy to fight. With one of his loved ones there, he could just close his eyes and rest, trusting that he would stand guard.

For the next several weeks, Jim did what he was told. He struggled to wake up, he struggled to eat, then he struggled to go back to sleep. The memory of how strong and self-assured he had been was lost in the fog of commands directed at him by the many people responsible for his care. As he followed the orders, a machine-like rhythm replaced the natural rhythm of his body. The robotic movements made him feel like a stranger, captive, within himself. Every once in a while, he would catch a glimpse of himself in the mirror and struggle to recognize the person looking back at him. The stranger's skin was pale; his muscles were melting away; his hair was glued to his head by sweat. Panic would rise up again, and the nurses would bring him medicine that helped him not to feel too much.

The drugs they gave him to tame his overwhelming pain helped him to detach himself from his body and tolerate the poking and prodding. He learned how to let his mind float far away while he was being manhandled. Sometimes he would find himself thinking it would be easier just to let go completely and not come back. But between the awful treatments, his mother and father would take turns crawling into bed with him and holding him. They would rub his arms, legs, and back, reminding him that his many parts were still attached to his body and that he was anchored in their unwavering love and support. He craved their touch because it kept him from leaving. He hated their touch because it kept him from leaving.

° ASSESSING — SELF, OTHERS, GOD °

Early in the morning, Jim would awaken to a team of doctors and residents huddled around his bed. He would listen to them discuss how clever they were for having saved his life. When Jim's parents arrived, he would be forced to tolerate more of the same. They called his progress a miracle and praised God. Both the doctors and his parents sounded grateful. Part of Jim felt he ought to be grateful. But gratitude was the last thing on his mind. His mind was singularly focused on getting better so he could get back to his life.

However, the reality of the situation was beginning to sink in. As the weeks went by, Jim began to ask questions and to get more involved in his care. This irritated some of the hospital staff. They wanted him to stay calm and compliant: life was easier for them that way. While his parents offered up prayers of devotion, Jim's instinct to strive for health made him more agitated and choleric. In suggesting that he pray, his parents thought they were offering him an opportunity to find peace. "Let go and let God," they said, but they did not understand that to him "letting go" was irrevocably linked to letting his guard down, giving in, giving up. The pull to give up was so strong, he had to scream to stay awake, to feel some semblance of control.

Control took the shape of demands. Jim demanded to be informed about the specifics of every treatment and that the doctors give him the straight goods on his prognosis. As he collected the information that all was not well, he waffled between verbally lashing out at whoever came near and retreating into himself. Anger would give way to sorrow, then shift back to anger again.

While the health-care team focused on the positive aspects of his care, Jim began to piece the facts together. He had injured his spine after landing awkwardly on the day he caught the football. He had damaged his spinal cord at T1. It was unlikely he would ever walk again. He would probably be in a wheelchair for the rest of his life.

With the bad news, Jim became ever more rigid in his approach. He began to form a hard, protective layer around his very being. He came and went; he did what he had to do. He tried hard not to think too far into the future.

Five months after his accident, Jim's physical health was stable enough for him to be transferred to a rehabilitation hospital. The transfer signaled progress, and Jim was determined not to be in rehab for long. Despite everything that he had been told, he still believed that hard work and the right medicine would help him get back to a productive, independent life. He would figure out what needed to be done and do it.

Jim went to the fitness rehabilitation center several times a day, taking every opportunity to do more than was expected. The rehab staff praised his determination. His parents were proud to see their son taking charge.

But at the end of his hard days, Jim would lie exhausted on the mat and the questions would start: How can I keep something like this from happening again? Did I deserve this? Why did God allow this to happen? Where the hell has God been all these months? The questions came at him in waves until he feared he would drown in their undertow. Panic would set in. The questions never brought him answers; they only served to confuse him, to draw energy away from his ability to focus on the job at hand.

It was becoming more obvious to Jim that no matter how hard he tried, his legs would not respond. His mood fluctuated between anger, self-pity, and disgust. He hated his body for failing him. He knew his family loved him. He knew they would never abandon him. But when he looked into their eyes and saw the pain his suffering was causing them, it was almost more than he could bear. He wished he were strong enough to push them away. He hated himself for needing them as much as he did.

His instinct was to fight, to take control, but in order to stay in control he could not afford the luxury of assessing philosophical questions. He was no longer free to wonder what great things God might have planned for him in the future. Now if he let his mind go even for a minute, he found himself gasping for breath. He used all of his energy to stay focused and turn the questions off. He began to turn away from anyone who talked about God; instead, he wrapped himself in a blanket of control.

Jim spent the next six months learning to work with the many therapists who were helping him address his long list of physical and psychological needs. The occupational therapists taught him how to adapt to his environment. The physiotherapists taught him how to manage life in a wheelchair. Jim attacked each problem as he always had: strategically, head on, with determination.

The hospital staff was well equipped to help Jim tackle the many psychological issues confronting him. With their help, he learned to discuss the anger brewing inside. He even accepted the necessity of attending group-counseling sessions. Although he had been determined to go it alone, he conceded that he might be able to learn something from the others who were there.

Wheeling into the group that first morning, Jim may as well have been carrying a white flag that spelled defeat. He was joining the club of those who were disabled. It was not a group he wanted to belong to. It was not a group he had grown up understanding or even respecting.

Until that point, he had been convinced he was special. Now, as he looked around the room, he could see he was no more special or deserving than anyone else. They had all been dealt a difficult hand. They had all worked hard to survive. They were more alike than different.

Over time, Jim learned a great deal about himself from the group sessions. He learned that the other patients' stories irritated him. He learned that he secretly delighted in someone else's explosion into anger. He learned that he didn't want to be as weak and pitiful as he considered them to be. He didn't want anyone to feel sorry for him, and he didn't feel like being empathetic with or sympathetic toward anyone else.

But it was through these interactions with the others that Jim began to see how guarded and inward facing he had become. In treatment they called it the "every man for himself syndrome." He learned how much more he needed to understand and to be understood. Although each person's story was unique, they shared a common bond. They had all been robbed of the opportunity to dream about what their lives might hold. Now their energies would have to narrowly focus on getting through the day as they navigated their world in wheelchairs.

Rehab taught him that he had been competing the way he always had, both with himself and others. Over time he began to learn how to be kind, both to himself and to the others struggling alongside him. He learned to see the value in them as unique individuals. They taught him to see the value in himself.

Nine months after the incident, Jim was discharged home with an excellent prognosis. He had superb support systems in place, and he was honest about his need for help. Outwardly, he appeared well prepared to manage his life as a paraplegic.

∘ Depression ∘

The family home had been successfully modified. The personal-care workers used a side entrance to access Jim's small apartment. Jim was able to maintain a certain level of independence. At first he was still hopeful that life would return to a normal rhythm. His friends dropped by to say hello and initially he was genuinely happy to visit with them.

Within a few weeks, however, Jim realized that things had changed more than he thought. When friends complained about day-to-day issues, he found himself annoyed by the superficiality of their conversation. He began to look at his friends and realize that he was somehow different. He was consumed by a sense of loneliness. While his friends worried about which movie they should attend, he worried about whether he could carry on living this way. He became aware of a deep and underlying anxiety that he could not reconcile or dissipate.

The more proficiently Jim lived the life of a paraplegic, the less able he was able to attribute his underlying anxiety to his physical disability. At first he thought it was part of adapting to his new physical surroundings, but as time went on, he began to realize that his physical status was only part of the cause.

Physically, his life was no longer in danger, but he was awake now to the fact that bad things can happen and when they did, not much could be done about it. He no longer knew or trusted himself. He knew he had been eating right and sleeping right and doing all the right things to stay healthy before his trauma.

But he was no longer under the spell of the health-care professionals who spoke to him about the odds, trying to reassure him that things would not get worse. He was awake now to the fact that they had no control over life's circumstances.

He no longer trusted a God who might not be there for him.

After all, where had God been when he hurt himself? In the hospital, there had been no message from God. God had not been at his shoulder, counseling him or holding him while he went through medical torture. On the many nights that he had pleaded with God, there had been no answer. He was coming to the dismal conclusion that there may not actually be a God. The bottom line for him was, if this could happen to him, then so could anything else — anytime, anyplace.

For a while he had fooled himself into believing that his hard work, determination, and resourcefulness had saved him, but he had seen others in the rehab hospital who had fought just as hard and were every bit as determined but had not been saved. He was coming to the conclusion that despite the best intentions of parents, family, and friends, despite his best efforts, despite access to the finest medicine, irrevocably bad things can happen, and when they did, there was no guarantee of a positive outcome.

He felt he was on the edge of a cliff he could fall off at any moment. During the initial part of rehabilitation, he had told himself that staying alive was a matter of free will. Now he felt that this perspective was both naïve and simplistic. No matter how hard he tried, he could no longer stop thinking about the big questions of life — Is there anyone who can save me? Can I save myself? — from flooding over him. He would fall into himself, with no idea of how to pull himself out of his deep funk.

He struggled with trying to forget about the experience of almost dying, but at the same time he was remarkably drawn to it. Again and again he would go over the same questions, until the chaos overwhelmed him. The questions linked together to form a chain that weighed him down in a way he had never experienced before. The weight traveled from his head right down through his whole body, making it hard for him to get up in the morning and even harder to fall asleep at night. When he tried to use the strategies he had been taught to lower his anxiety, he would fall even deeper into himself. He tried to talk to his family, but it was obvious they could not help him. They were exhausted by the whole ordeal and in hindsight in need of counseling themselves. They were happy he was home; happy the trauma was over; happy to be getting their own lives back to normal.

The only label Jim could apply to his struggle was "'depression,'" so he tried the cocktail of treatments that had been suggested in the hospital. He tried the medications, the meditations, the prayers, the biofeedback. All would take the edge off for a brief time, but the state of being quiet and relaxed only served to bring back memories of the deep peace he had felt when lying on the football field looking up at an exquisite blue sky. He would find himself strangely drawn to it. And then he would panic again.

Jim had been wishing he could go back to his old life. Now he knew he could never believe in the goodness of life the way he had before. The belief that he could go through life controlling death had been shattered. His innocence was gone. He was supposed to be happy he was not dead, but he felt as though he *were* dead. He was on a bridge trying desperately to get back to where he came from, while somehow knowing that he was never going back. He was standing there swaying in the wind, not knowing how to get away from death. He was alone. He began to think about ending it all.

Death began to preoccupy him. Why bother having things or doing things when one day you were going to be dead? Why bother fighting this hard every day when ultimately you're going to end up: dead? Death was there when he opened his eyes in the morning: he would pause for a moment to make sure he was alive. Death was there when he closed his eyes at night: he would think about having seen his loved ones for the last time. Lifelong learning had taught him to run from any thoughts of death. Yet now the prospect of being with death seemed comforting, logical, and attractive. He found himself in the very center of the enemy camp.

∘ EPIPHANY OF DESPAIR ∘

Until then, Jim had been convinced he could pull himself back from the brink of death whenever he wanted. He believed his God would help him stay safe. He had fooled himself into thinking he could control death; that his determination and good behavior had afforded him the luxury of sending death on its way. Now he was beginning to realize that death had not gone away. Death had shown its face and then simply stepped aside for the moment. He had been under the illusion that if he tried really hard, things would be fine. Now he was awake to the fact that he did not have that much control in life. His body could break down at any moment. Even if he did all the right things, bad things could still happen. His own mortality had become all too real.

Coming to terms with death meant relinquishing any notion of control, but control was the only lever Jim knew how to pull. He was afraid to let go of it, because by letting go he might be embracing death.

The distress he was feeling began to make sense as he realized what he was afraid of: that he was going to die one day and nothing was going to change that; that with or without a God, there was no way to avoid or control death. Worse, he could see himself willingly going to death. He was beginning to understand death as a part of life. In those moments of despair, when nothing was the way that it had been and everything and everyone seemed part of a play he could not comprehend, Jim began to understand how different his paradigm had become. He was beginning to suspect that death was in fact part of life and that life was directly interwoven with death. The clarity with which he was beginning to see his world unfold both terrified him and exhilarated him. He was left inarticulate in its significance.

Jim tried to tell his loved ones how he was feeling. But anytime he brought the topic up, they looked worried and tried to distract him. They told him in many different ways not to speak of death. They did not look at him when he spoke of it. They stood away from him and stroked him. They patted him on the shoulder, the back, or the head; they did not come into his body the way they had in the hospital. They said things like, "Thank God those days are behind us now," or "Let's focus on the positive."

He tried to discuss these feelings with his doctors, but to them, conversations about death spelled danger and defeat and they immediately referred him back to the rehabilitation psychiatrist with a diagnosis of depression. The psychiatrist spoke to him about post-traumatic stress and prescriptions that would help him forget.

Out of desperation, he sought the counsel of his minister. He had been hoping that he had missed something; that there was a way for him to understand why God had not come to his aid; that maybe he had the whole thing wrong; that maybe there was a reason for feeling abandoned by God. As he tried to talk to his minister about his preoccupation with death, the minister suggested that he pray for peace. But Jim wondered, how peaceful is it to think that I am all alone and have no control over death?

He needed to talk about death, but the experts he consulted did not know how to let him do that. To them, talking about death meant he was sick, and their job was to help him stay clear of the topic. To Jim, not thinking about death meant believing in the illusion that we have control in life.

It was important for him to explore his new feelings. He could no longer believe the way he once had. Blind faith in a just world was no longer an option. Part of him felt like a victim because he was alone; the other part of him was finally able to see that none of the experts had power over death. He wondered why they could not see that. He wondered if they were all that naïve. The more he thought about it, the more he began to realize what he was up against. He knew more, not less, than the experts did.

His loss of innocence carried with it an insight that helped him explore his thoughts on the topic. He began to ask himself, what the hell was I thinking? Of course I'm going to die one day. Of course I am not happy about it. Of course no one else wants to talk about it: they *are* going to die, too! It *is* depressing. Jim would find himself oscillating between fear and a sense of relief.

◦ ACCEPTANCE ◦

Jim was beginning to glimpse a universal truth about life. He was beginning to understand why he felt so alone. The more he thought about it, the more he knew it was true. Death is real. Whether life ends now or later was just a matter of the details.

The many health therapists and religious people he had met in the year since his accident had all talked about acceptance. Jim had struggled with the word, frequently asking himself, accept what? Accept that this is God's will? Accept that I should feel a certain way? That I should settle? He had been concerned that the word meant he would be giving up his desire to fight. He had vowed never to give up; never to stop trying to improve his circumstances. But now for the first time he understood the word quite differently.

He could see that acceptance was not the same as resignation or surrender. To accept actually meant to simply acknowledge the reality of life. Acceptance didn't mean being passive in the face of physical limitations or in the face of God's plan; it meant acknowledging the reality that life does include death. The way Jim figured it, he had three choices.

Say he'd had enough and end it all right then.

Take the drugs for depression and pretend none of what he was learning was true.

Accept life the way it really is, with no guarantees.

◦ ACQUIRING RESOURCES — SELF, OTHERS, GOD ◦

In the late fall, Jim attended a play with his family. It was a major milestone for all of them. With the help of his attendant, he arranged his own transportation and met his family at the door of the theater. His parents hovered over him, scarcely believing their son was independent again. Jim beamed with pride at the significance of his accomplishment. They entered the theater together and proceeded to their special seats.

When the lights dimmed and the curtain was drawn, a powerful calmness came over him. The words he had been searching for came to him, and he was able to describe how he had been feeling over the last few months.

He had been bothered by all the people he knew who were absorbed in their own story lines: stories about their cars, their homes, their quests for personal wealth. It bothered him how these things seemed to hypnotize them. Now, as he watched people settle into their seats at the theater, he realized that he saw his own life as a play: one where he knew the ending. He found himself understanding why superficial issues bothered him so much. Each and every day, people were taking the stage and pretending everything they did was real, when in the end none of it mattered. Everyone ended up the same: face-to-face with death. Jim found himself fighting the temptation to shout, "Don't you know you don't really have any control? That this is all an illusion? We are all going to be dead one day!"

As he sat there in the dark, he looked around the room. He looked at his family, who seemed happy to be enjoying the illusion unfolding on the stage. He looked at all the people enjoying themselves. He was reminded of the days when he did not know. He realized in that moment that he did not want to take the joy away from those who were watching the show. He did not want to make others learn what he now knew to be true. He also realized that he did not want to continue to live the way he had been living: never really enjoying the play of life just because he knew the ending. In that moment, he realized that shattering the illusion might hurt others, but by fearing death, he had been hurting himself.

In that moment, he made a commitment to himself to get up every morning and participate wholeheartedly in the play of life. He would try to get as much learning out of each day as he possibly could, so that when the play ended and it was time for him to go to death, he would have been part of a great performance.

The choice he made taught him about the kind of person he wanted to be and the people he wanted to continue to cherish. As he looked at his friends and family, he was consumed with gratitude for having even just a few more moments with them. He was truly humbled by the opportunity he had been given to live.

He asked if maybe there was a God. It was a question he was careful not to answer, but he knew that in asking the question, he was acknowledging that there might be things he did not understand. No longer was it his ego talking; it was a powerful force that allowed him to wonder what life might hold. Finally he knew the difference between striving for outcomes and strategically acquiring resources that might help him live a happy, fulfilled life. He had been elevated to a higher plane and life had never been sweeter or his path clearer. He shed the cynical thick outer skin he had developed following his accident. What was exposed was the natural brilliance of his soul.

PERCEIVED THREAT

Christine's Story

Reconciling death is an important part of healthy living, and yet our Western society encourages us to believe in the illusion that life and death are separate. While this naïve perspective might provide comfort to an individual, it does so only to the point at which that person becomes aware of death.

Awareness that death is real can come to anyone, at any time. Even the perception of a threat is often all it takes. One thing that remains constant is that when the awareness of death comes, the elephant in the room can no longer be ignored. Naïvety is no longer an option.

To learn to live with death, we must first see it. We must come to know that it is real. We must admit once and for all that we are mortal and that one day life as we know it will end. Far from being the end point, learning that death is real offers us the opportunity for a new beginning.

Christine's story reinforces how the awareness of death, though it can be hard to see, can come to us at any time and in any place.

The Toronto airport was busy, loud, and crowded. Harried travelers rushed from ticket booths to gates, dragging huge suitcases behind them. But Christine sat in a world of her own.

America at its best, she thought as she looked down at her ticket. That's what her mother had called Washington, D.C., and she herself dimly remembered a lovely and interesting city, although the memory, belonging to a family trip, was twenty years old.

Suddenly she felt a sense of trepidation. Recent events had made traveling to destinations like Washington a decidedly somber experience. She tried not to think about that. Instead she focused on doing everything she could to make the trip enjoyable.

Like getting herself a four-dollar caffe latte — why not? Christine walked over to the Starbucks counter and ordered herself a cup — something she didn't often do, but today was all about treating herself. She was determined not to let any more negative thoughts break into her perfect day.

Coffee in hand, she sauntered over to the check-in counter. The man at the desk looked up just long enough to read her ticket. "Washington?" he said.

"Yes," she said. Then, hesitantly, she asked, "I was wondering about this upgrade certificate?" She placed a piece of paper on the counter.

After tapping at his computer a few times, the man announced with a wide smile that she could indeed be upgraded to the business-class section. His eyes now met hers — in fact, Christine thought his whole demeanor had changed. Or maybe it was her imagination, for she was now feeling a bit smug. She had never traveled business class before. Armed with her delicious latte and shiny new upgraded ticket, she threw her shoulders back and headed toward U.S. Customs.

The line at Customs was long. "Longer than usual," she overheard the distinguished-looking man in front of her saying.

After Customs, Christine had to navigate extra security checkpoints. She walked a very long way through the terminal to a different boarding gate, where she had to take out her passport and ticket again. This time it was checked by an armed guard. There was little in the way of conversation. Everything was deadly serious. Finally, once security was assured, or so they said, Christine was allowed to board.

She waited for thirty minutes in her comfortable seat, looking from her window at the people scurrying on the runway below, until the speaker gave a loud crackle and a woman's voice announced the plane would not be leaving as planned. A chorus of groans and sighs from the other passengers accompanied the announcement. The stewardess gave an explanation, one Christine could not make out. An announcement came over the speaker demanding that all passengers stay in their seats. Hearing that she was trapped made Christine toy with the idea of making a run for it. She laughed at the ridiculousness of her thought. She reminded herself they were just being extra careful.

She took a fashion magazine out of her bag. "Red is the hot new color for spring," she read, and then read again. She just couldn't concentrate. After a few minutes, she thrust the magazine aside. She smiled at the young woman next to her, but neither felt much like talking.

Finally, after an hour had passed, the speaker burst into life again: "We are now ready for take off." Christine settled back in her comfortable seat. At last, she thought, all is well.

Once the plane was aloft, everyone seemed to relax. The steward and stewardess offered her a smorgasbord of delicious food choices. As she took another bite of her dessert, she wondered if the people in the back knew what they were missing.

The man and woman sitting on either side of her began to talk, first to each other, and then to her. Christine was enjoying the company, enjoying the atmosphere, enjoying a good meal and a smooth flight.

"So then my wife said —" the man was saying, when the speakers crackled to life again.

The plane would be performing an emergency landing. This time, no explanation was given. Christine sat up straight and looked to the front of the plane, where she could see the stewardesses huddled together, whispering. The man beside Christine had gone pale.

She sank deeper into her seat, her heart about to burst. She thought about standing up, but where would she go? Where could she run? To curb her growing terror, she tried to focus on her breathing. Breathe deeply, she told herself, her hand pressed against her chest. But it was getting harder to breathe, and even harder to think. Chris felt the air pressure in the cabin begin to fall.

The oxygen masks tumbled down from the ceiling and she struggled to put hers over her mouth. It was clear the plane was headed down. She tried to remember the flight path. Were they flying over water? Did she need a life-vest? Where did they say it was? She frantically searched under the seat and pulled it out. She looked out the window of the plane and in the distance could see another plane drawing near. Oh, my God! she thought, tears stinging her eyes. This can't be happening. Screams flooded the plane.

She thought about using her cellphone to call her husband and children. What would she say? She thought about all the people who had called their families on September 11. She understood now how much courage it must have taken for them to say goodbye. But after imagining her family's reaction to the news, she just didn't think she could do it. Instead, she fumbled in her purse, desperately trying to remember where she had put the picture of her family. Money, cards, notes — all the detritus of a life now seemingly over — fell to the floor as she struggled to locate the only thing she truly valued. Finally her fingers found the picture and she gave it one last glance before she tucked it inside her dress. She wished she could pray, or scream, or do something, but nothing came to her. She just sat there holding her hands over the picture she had buried in the fold of clothing over her heart.

The captain's voice came over the speaker. The planes, he said, had been sent to escort them to their landing. The Air Force had arrived. Some continued to scream through their oxygen masks, while others wept. Chris sat there observing and listening, as if watching a play unfold in front of her.

· SURVIVING ·

Christine's head felt heavy. A dull pain assaulted her eyes when she tried to drag her lids open. The morning light, soft and pale in the hotel room, felt like a searing hot neon blaze. When she was able to open her eyes without flinching, she was greeted by Ron's touch. It took her a few moments to remember the plane, the oxygen masks, the weeping of the other passengers. When she did, she sat straight up in the bed and jerked herself out of her husband's embrace, struggling to breathe.

Ron tried to pull her close again. "Honey?" he said.

She moved out from under the covers to the edge of the bed and crossed her legs.

She scanned her memory files and came up with a series of images, none of which seemed to be connected. She remembered that the plane had landed one hundred miles away from Washington and that there had been buses to the Capital. She remembered getting off her bus, but had no memory of leaving the plane. She wondered about the picture of her family. What had she done with it? She thought about the other people who were on the plane and couldn't remember if she had said good-bye to them.

She remembered seeing Ron standing, waiting for her — but had that been at the hotel or the airport? She scrunched up her face and closed her eyes, holding her head in her hands, trying to piece together the evening's events.

"I feel like it was all a dream I can't quite remember," she said, not looking at him.

"I'm sure you had a real fright, sweetheart, but everything's fine, thank God." Ron put his hand on her back. "You're here. You're safe."

Christine thought for a moment about the word "safe."

She lay back down on the bed, a little stiffly. Yes, I should be happy I'm safe, she thought. The plane didn't crash. No one was hurt. I'm alive.

After a few minutes, Christine had to sit up again. She pulled away from her husband. This time he sat up, too. He tried to take her into his arms, but she resisted. "I need to go over what happened last night," she said.

Ron explained that a male passenger on the plane had made some kind of threat. Nobody would tell him who the man was or what he had said, but the two air marshals flying undercover had made quick work of him. Airline personnel described the whole incident as minor. In landing the plane as dramatically as they had, they were simply following airline security protocol. Ron told her everything had proceeded smoothly, considering what might have happened. Escorted by the military, her plane had landed safely, and neither she nor any other passenger had been harmed.

"Everything is fine," he said.

He's right, she thought. Everything is fine.

Ron told her that earlier in the morning he had called the children to see if anyone at home had heard about the incident. "But they hadn't," he said. "Nothing at all." He had scanned the newspapers and television news reports to see if anyone would mention it. None had. "The only people who seem to know about this are the ones who were directly involved." He sounded sure it would make Christine's life easier if the whole incident were forgotten, as if nothing had ever happened — as if her perfect day had been as perfect as she'd first envisioned it that morning in the airport.

Christine's heart began to race. A sick, sad feeling bubbled up in her chest. Her memories of what had happened were still raw and painful. Ron, noticing the look on her face, softened his tone and asked her if she wanted to go home or if she would prefer to stay in Washington and attempt to enjoy herself, despite everything that had happened.

Pull yourself together, Christine told herself. "You're right, Ron," she said. "Let's just forget anything ever happened."

He nodded. "You need a vacation from work and the kids. A few nice dinners with friends will have you feeling good as new." He kissed her cheek and went into the washroom, where he began to shave.

Yes, Ron was right, Christine thought. Why be so upset over

something that hadn't even happened? The story could be simplified and pared down into nothing more frightening than an interesting story she would tell the kids someday.

Amy and John greeted Christine and Ron with huge grins and hugs when they walked into the café for brunch later that morning. Christine took a seat next to Amy, who immediately poured Christine a cup of coffee from the big pot they had already ordered. "How was your flight?" she asked brightly.

Christine took a deep breath for the first time since the incident. She was happy to be asked. She paused, with the intention of organizing her thoughts. Where would she start? How much should she tell? But by the time she opened her mouth to speak, the conversation had moved on. She looked around the table and realized that her friend was just being polite. Amy didn't really want to know. Christine looked over at Ron, who was engrossed in ordering breakfast from the menu. Her chest tightened as the memories of how she had felt on the plane came flooding back. The restaurant was crowded, and her friends and husband boisterous and affectionate, but she felt so alone.

The waitress interrupted her. "Day dreaming?" she said.

"Just a rough night," Christine said.

"Oh, I get it," the waitress replied with a wink, looking significantly at Ron. Everyone laughed.

That was enough to snap Christine out of it. She ordered herself French toast with whipped cream and strawberries — after all, didn't she deserve a treat? She engaged herself in planning the day's events.

Several times over the course of the next few days, Christine thought about sharing her experience with her friends, but everytime she opened her mouth, she was unable to find the words to describe what she had felt. Finally, at brunch in their hotel's restaurant on Sunday, the final day of their stay, the conversation lagged for a moment. Christine decided this might be the time to broach the subject.

"So I had quite the flight in," she began, laughing nervously. She went over the details of the unscheduled landing

Amy gasped. "Why didn't you say anything before, Chris?" she asked.

Christine was tempted to remind them that she had tried to share the story the day before, but she didn't have the energy.

"What happened next?" Amy asked.

Christine's voice began to shake and she fell silent for a moment, twisting her napkin in her hands.

Trying to save her the embarrassment of revealing her emotions, Ron tried to fill in the details of the landing. Soon the conversation shifted course. Amy, John, and Ron each had a story to tell about airport security, airplane scares, national defense, and the reasons those in charge kept these things quiet. The superficiality of the conversation irritated her. Wasn't anyone going to ask her how she felt? She grew quiet and pushed her plate aside. When the waitress passed by the table, she ordered herself a glass of wine.

"With brunch?" Ron asked with a laugh.

"Sure," she said. "I'm on vacation, right?"

Christine sat back in the chair and enjoyed her Sauvignon.

As the first sip trickled down her throat, she felt it stick for a moment to the lump that had been there since her ordeal began. Then the wine slid over the lump and down into her chest. Every sip thereafter felt like she was running warm water over where she had held the picture of her family, slowly washing away that memory of pain. For the first time since the incident, she could feel her body relax.

By the time brunch ended, Christine had managed to soothe herself quite well, and her friends thought it was funny to see her finally looking so at ease. Christine even made a joke about expecting the flight home to be a little more boring than the flight in. Ron looked relieved that she was able to talk about the flight home at all. He was worried that boarding another plane would be difficult for her.

The group met again at five and took the shuttle to the airport. Christine, still feeling the effects of her liquid lunch, didn't mention her recent flight, nor did her husband or her friends. Instead, the couples laughed about the multitude of household tasks awaiting them at home, and confirmed their commitment to meet at the same time next year.

"It was great seeing you!" Amy called as she and Ron headed toward their gate.

"Call me soon!" Christine replied with a smile. She noted with relief that she was back to feeling normal. Sure, she was a little sad to have to say goodbye to her friends, but she was also happy to have spent some time with them. Ron took her hand and they wheeled their luggage to the gate.

Christine continued to chatter away as they boarded the plane. She handed her boarding card to her husband and let him take the lead. When they got to their seats, she set her things down, but kept chatting.

"Ma'am, could you please buckle your seatbelt?" the steward-ess said as she made the rounds.

Christine turned pale. Trapped, she thought. Trapped again.

As the plane taxied on the runway, beads of sweat formed on her brow. She struggled to catch her breath.

Ron squeezed her hand, which lay cold and limp in his own.

"I think I'm going to be sick," Christine told him thickly.

"Chris, wait —" Ron said, but she ripped open her seatbelt and staggered toward the bathroom.

The stewardess's voice was harsh as she ordered Christine to sit down.

"I … I — " Christine protested.

Ron grabbed her and pulled her back into the seat. "Sit down. It will just be a minute."

She still wasn't able to catch her breath — it was as if she were breathing through a straw. "I have to get off the plane," she told Ron. Her hands were shaking.

"Put your head down," Ron said. "Just close your eyes and breathe. Nice slow, deep breaths, nice slow deep breaths …" He began breathing with her.

When Christine opened her eyes again, after what seemed like an eternity of terror, she was met by the stares of all the sur-rounding passengers.

Christine pulled the magazine she had bought at the airport out of her bag and hid her face behind it.

"I'm so sorry. I just don't know what came over me," she told Ron, who was slumped, exhausted, in his seat. Christine thought to examine her feelings in more detail, but she told herself that once she had her feet firmly planted back on the ground and could hold her children again, she would feel normal. Everything would be fine. Ron, for his part, seemed happy to let the conversation go. Not another word was exchanged between them.

When the plane landed, Christine and Ron rushed to be among the first ones out. Without much discussion, they decided to pay the extra for an airport limousine rather than wait for a cab. As the driver carried them away, Christine pressed her face to the window and watched the city, her home, come into view.

She imagined what her mother would say about her behavior on the plane. "Don't be ridiculous," she would tell her. "Snap out of it! You're lucky everything has turned out so well. You do realize that nothing actually happened!"

Christine attempted a smile in Ron's direction.

The car pulled up to her house, and Christine could see her children — Tommy, eight, and Charlotte, ten — waiting in the window. Tommy was jumping up and down with excitement. Christine jumped out of the limo, almost before it had fully stopped, and ran into the house, scooping up both children in a big hug. Finally, she thought, I'm home.

The following morning, Christine resumed her responsibilities.

After waking up at the normal time, she got the children off to school, and then rushed through traffic to work. It was difficult to get back into the swing of things. That was the part of being away on holidays that she hated. It seemed to her that the better the trip, the harder it was for her to re-enter normal life: to drive her own car, to make her own coffee, to focus on the pile of work that sat in front of her. So feeling that she could barely get through the day did not seem unusual.

She even laughed about it with her friends at work. "I just can't figure out where my staff is today. I was expecting my breakfast, and my limo driver, and they didn't show up!" They all laughed together. When they asked about her trip, Christine was happy to share the drama of her flight there. She made absolutely no mention of the trip home. The reaction that she got from her colleagues was exactly the same as from her friends in Washington: an initial gesture of sympathy and then a whole round of commentary on airport security. Christine did not bother trying to make her point. She did not really know what her point was. After all, she was home; she was safe. Nothing had happened.

The next few weeks, Christine was busy preparing for the holidays. There were the children's school concerts. There was baking to be done and the house to be decorated. There were gifts to buy and deadlines at work. Christine lay out a schedule for herself and tried the best she could to stick to it. The only time she felt a little relief was when she and Ron attended their various holiday receptions and she had a few glasses of wine. Only then could she feel herself let go a little bit. Only then could she feel herself taking a very deep breath, the kind of breath that makes one want to sigh as it is exhaled.

When morning finally came, Christine would find herself begging for just a few more minutes of sleep. At night, when Ron would try to hold her, she would tell him she just too exhausted. She told herself if she could get the holidays over, everything would get back to normal.

∘ ASSESSING — SELF, OTHERS, GOD ∘

As the number of days before the holidays shortened, Christine found her symptoms getting worse. Not only was she exhausted all the time, but she was having stomachaches and occasional headaches. One morning, after she crawled into work, she picked up the phone and made an appointment to be seen in the clinic downstairs.

The nurse booking the appointment suggested she take a few minutes to list her symptoms before coming in the next day. Christine closed her office door, took a notepad out of her desk drawer, and began to write. It was easy for her to describe the physical symptoms: the heartburn, the trips to the bathroom, the waves of nausea, the lack of energy, the trouble sleeping. She had a little more trouble describing her mood. Clearly she was irritable. She knew this was true at the office, as well as at home. She wondered whether she was getting to the age where hormones were beginning to wreak havoc, or whether her symptoms were more serious. Did she have cancer, or was she just suffering from her busy life as a working mother? Was she dying or did she have Crazy Mom Syndrome?

The clinic was busy, full of people who looked just like she did. Exhausted. The plight of the working parent, just trying to have it all, she thought. The doctor did a series of tests. When he discovered the tenderness over her abdomen, he said he would test her for irritable bowel syndrome. IBS, he called it, explaining it was the most common gastrointestinal diagnosis worldwide. "An estimated 13% to 20% of North Americans have IBS," he said, "and it is significantly more common in women than in men." He suggested they do some investigative tests in the New Year and gave her a list of foods to be avoided. He made mention of her busy life and suggested she get some rest over the holidays.

Finally Christine had a reason for her symptoms. Thank God she wasn't dying. She committed to taking better care of herself and went back to work. The combination of her new diagnosis and the stress from the holidays clearly accounted for her unusual symptoms. She knew she was overreacting to things, particularly as they related to the children's safety. Now she could see that their comings and goings were just adding too many variables to an already full place. She convinced herself that she wanted them close so she did not have to worry about them.

The holidays came and went and with them Christine's reason for being off balance. It seemed she felt her old self only after a few glasses of wine. Only then could she feel herself get out from under the weight of impending doom. Without the wine, she would find herself worrying about everything. Sometimes she wouldn't allow Charlotte to go to a friend's house, just to keep her close and safe. Then, on the rare occasions that she gave the kids permission to go out with their friends, she would sit by the phone, her stomach in knots, and wait for them to call. She did the same with Ron, calling him two or three times a day.

She woke up a few times every night in the grip of panic: her heart would be racing; she'd have difficulty breathing. Ron would reach over and coax her to lie down. Sometimes that was enough to make the feeling go away, but other times she would lie there for a long time in the darkness, thinking about everything that could go wrong. She would imagine vivid, nightmarish scenarios. Sometimes her family was in a car accident. Other times they had fallen prey to a horrible disease. Occasionally she would think about the incident on the plane. How scared she was, how alone she was.

And then she would get angry. Angry at the way people reacted to her story. Angry that they were so interested in the unimportant details. "What airline was it?" "Where was the plane headed?" Or "How many people were on board?" Why wasn't anybody asking the right questions? She stopped telling anyone about it.

These thoughts would continue until the alarm clock went off and she would drag herself to the bathroom to wash her face, careful not to look too closely at her haggard, ravaged reflection.

One mid-January morning as she arrived outside the office, she found herself sitting in her car in the parking lot, hardly able to move, wondering how she was going to muster up the strength to make it through the day. She lifted a wan hand to undo her seatbelt, and let it drop. She did this three times before she was finally able to gather up enough energy to let herself out of the car.

Later, in a meeting, when one of the company's accountants was discussing their latest earning period, she was overwhelmed by a wave of nausea so powerful she had to put her head between her knees and pretend to riffle through her bag. And when Janie, manager of the sales department, burst into her office and asked how her children were enjoying being back at school, Christine snapped that she was too busy to talk.

"Oh … I'm sorry," Janie said. She stood there for a moment awkwardly, then walked out of the office, closing the door gently behind her.

Chris felt guilty and began to compose an e-mail apology, but gave it up after five minutes. Everything seemed to take so much energy. She would explain it all to Janie later. Not today. She was simply too tired.

But the feelings didn't go away the next day, or the day after that. Christine would find herself counting the minutes until she could go home and grab that bottle of wine out of the kitchen, sit back on the couch, and have a glass or two.

It was becoming harder for her to convince herself that she was just over-tired. And harder for Ron to ignore her drinking.

"You certainly seem to be enjoying your wine these days," he said, with a laugh that to her was clearly false.

"Oh come on, Ron," she said. "It's a good transition from

work. It sets the mood for a more relaxing evening. Don't you want me relaxed? You keep telling me how stressed I look."

When she was sitting in her room later that evening, Christine overheard her husband say to Tommy and Charlotte, "Just give your mother whatever she wants. She's very tired."

Christine stomped into the hallway. "Has it occurred to you how condescending you sound?" she yelled into his shocked face. "You're not trying to help me," she said. "You're trying to silence me." Her steady stream of screams pierced every wall in the house.

Back in bed, Christine, calmer now, wondered what had happened to her. It had been years since she had lost control like that. She could still see the look of terror on Tommy and Charlotte's faces. Thank God Ron had sent them to their room to protect them from the madwoman who had taken control of their home. Ron had tried to reason with her, battling to keep his voice low and steady. When she had continued to yell at him, he had turned his back on her and gone down to the basement.

Christine wished she could undo the mess she had made. She wished she could pray for some divine insight. She decided to go back to the clinic the next day.

When she woke up the next morning, she was happy to feel Ron's body beside hers. She rolled over to face him — but he had turned away from her. It was hard for her to know where to begin, and for a while she just looked at him, feeling a hundred emotions. Christine was still angry at his patronizing attitude in front of the kids, but she had to concede she had completely overreacted.

"I'm going to see a doctor today," she said. "I think I've come down with something and that's why I acted the way I did last night — and, well, lately."

Without turning toward her, Ron said, "Good. You haven't been yourself since that trip to Washington."

Christine didn't reply. Despite her hurt feelings, she knew he was right, but hearing it stated so bluntly left her with a lot to think about. It was true she hadn't been well since she had gone to Washington. She would find out what was wrong and somehow get it fixed.

Sitting at a silent kitchen table with her family later that morning, Christine wasn't sure what tack to take with the children. Should she begin by apologizing for her outburst, or explain that she wasn't feeling well? Would it be better for the children to think their mother was sick, or that she had gone crazy? Sickness was easier to explain, she thought, so she led off with a list of physical symptoms.

"But don't worry, because I'm going to see a doctor today," she concluded.

The children remained quiet. but looked relieved. Christine gave them tighter hugs than usual before they left to catch the bus for school.

At lunchtime Christine decided to go to her yoga class at the nearby community center. She hadn't been for months, but no matter how busy the day, if she could get herself there, she was always happy with the results.

Christine stood near the back of the class. She knew she always had trouble performing even basic moves when she was out of practice. As the instructor, Marci, urged the class to salute the sun, her mind raced through the list of things she had to do that day. All the more reason to be here, she thought, trying to focus on the instructions.

As Christine lay on her mat at the end of class, Marci came by to cover her with a blanket. All hell broke loose.

Christine sat up and began to hyperventilate. The memory of the plane and the feeling of being trapped came flooding back. Marci kneeled beside her, stroking her back and murmuring words of comfort that Christine could barely hear. Thinking she might be sick, Christine scrambled to her feet and ran out of the class. Marci caught up to her in the hall. Christine, panting, sat against the wall and hugged her knees to her chest.

After a few minutes, she recovered enough to try to explain her strange behavior. "I'm just a little stressed," she said. Even as she said it, she knew her excuse sounded weak.

"Clearly your body is reacting to more than a little stress," Marci said. "Something very significant is going on for you. I suggest you try to find out what that is. Find out what it is. Learn from it." She rubbed Christine's back and breathed with her before going back into the classroom.

∘ DEPRESSION ∘

Christine sat alone in the dark, quiet hallway. Tears streamed down her face. She found no comfort in Marci's words. She knew she was right. There was definitely something going on here — something terrible going on inside her — but she had no idea what it was. She thought about the incident with her family the night before and her complete loss of control. Was she having some kind of breakdown? Was she sick? There's only one thing I'm sure of, she thought, and it's that I'm absolutely petrified.

Christine drove back to work, turning up the volume on the radio to drown out any negative thoughts. I'm going to keep it simple, she told herself. She would see the doctor tomorrow. He would tell her what was wrong. She would do whatever needed to be done to get better. In the meantime, there would be no feeling sorry for herself, no mind games, no meditating on her plight, no more introspection. She would be a machine.

When she got home that afternoon, she greeted her family in the same way she might welcome a good friend with whom she'd recently had a heated argument. She was warm and charming, but held back a bit in case the toxic soup bubbling inside her spilled over. None of them deserved to be treated badly. She would get herself fixed tomorrow. Like taking a car in need of repair to the shop, she thought wryly. She sat down and made the appropriate maternal sounds as her children told her about their day.

When Ron got home, he was ready to accept her apology for the previous evening. They enjoyed a nice family dinner — complete with a few glasses of wine, of course. Christine sat back in her chair, just as she had done with her friends in Washington, and listened to Ron and the children talk. She didn't mention the yoga class.

By the next morning, she had half convinced herself that another trip to the doctor was no longer necessary. For once, she had slept well, without any bad dreams or insomnia. She had almost forgotten her outburst. But remembering the twenty-four-hour cancellation fee, she reluctantly decided to show up at the clinic.

The nurse greeted Christine with a series of questions and handed her a pile of forms, with rows and rows of potential symptoms to be checked off. With a sigh, Christine sat on the uncomfortable waiting-room chair and went down the list. It was difficult to explain her problem. Did she have heart problems? Well, no, her palpitations hardly qualified as severe cardiac symptoms. She did suffer from gastro-intestinal problems, but with the new medication, the nausea seemed to lessening. Headaches came and went throughout the day. Had there been a category for over-dramatic basket case, she would have gladly ticked it off.

The doctor called her into his office a few minutes later. He bombarded her with another series of questions. Christine answered no to all of them. Finally, he stared at her through his thick glasses and asked, "Why did you come here?"

Christine began to cry. She didn't know what to say.

"Are you having trouble at home? Are you unhappy in your marriage?" he asked.

"I don't know," she replied, tears falling into her lap. "I don't think so."

"Work stressful?" he continued.

None of the questions seemed to hit the mark. Was she unhappy in her marriage? No, Ron was a good man. She knew she still loved him. But at the moment he wasn't able to offer her comfort. Was she feeling stressed at work? In general she liked her job, but lately she would find herself sitting at her desk, ignoring her overflowing inbox and wondering whether all of her paper pushing had any significance in the grand scheme of things.

Christine recounted her husband's comment that she had been having these symptoms since her trip to Washington several months before. She told the doctor about the plane. And then she sat and waited.

The doctor finally broke the silence. He said she might want to consider seeing someone to help her deal with her stress. His tone had grown kinder. "In some patients," he said, "the physical symptoms can mask an underlying psychological problem like anxiety. Perhaps the trip on the plane has caused you more psychological trauma than you thought."

He explained it was not all uncommon for people to react weeks or months later as they struggle to cope with the feeling that they have lost control. "This loss of control can put a person in a state of extreme confusion and insecurity. We call it Post Traumatic Stress Disorder. A person with PTSD may withdraw from friends and family; they may lose interest in activities and have difficulty with intimacy."

She listened carefully as he told her that apart from anxiety itself, psychological symptoms could include irritability, difficulty in concentration, and restlessness. Physical symptoms might include heart palpitations, sweating, nausea, and diarrhea," he said. "You could also experience some difficulty in breathing, as well as dizziness and headaches."

"I guess that sounds about right," she said. "So what now?"

He suggested she get started on a course of short-term drugs to help her deal with the anxiety. Then, on the way out of the office, he gave her the name of a few psychologists who specialized in PTSD.

Christine walked back to her office with a prescription for medicine in one hand and the name of a doctor for "crazy people" in the other. She knew better than to discuss any of this with her friends at work. She decided to fill the prescription for the medication, and sought out a psychologist who was far from where she worked. All she needed was for her boss to think she was having some kind of breakdown.

Over the next few weeks, Christine began to feel a little better. Clearly the medication was working and the cognitive behavioral treatment she was involved with was helping keep her in check. She worked hard to control her obsessive behaviors and thoughts of impending doom.

Things that needed to get done got done. Nothing more, nothing less. The chaos inside her could wait. The children came and went. They checked in with their requests and were seldom denied. Ron came and went, too. She didn't ask him where he was going anymore, or what time he would be home. A few times he invited her to come and sit with him, to listen to some music he'd bought for her. She would sit down only for a minute, a smile plastered on her face, and then think of some excuse to be off again. Did he want some tea? Was that someone at the door? Was one of the children calling?

Christine felt she was coming around, but the truth was that things were getting worse, not better.

Christine read the newspaper from front to back, ignoring any feel-good articles. She scanned instead for stories of people who had suffered: orphaned children, starving infants, an old man caught in a terrible fire. She cried for all of them, her head pressed against the kitchen table, her hand over her mouth so her family wouldn't hear.

One morning, she could not get out of bed. Every time she opened her eyes, the room swirled around as if she were looking at it through a kaleidoscope, and waves of nausea would overtake her. Ron sat on the edge of the bed helplessly watching her struggle.

"The flu," she said. "I've just got the flu."

Ron tried to lie down beside her to offer some comfort, but she quickly ushered him out, telling him someone needed to take care of the children. She tried not to notice the wounded look in his eyes as he headed off to the shower.

When Ron came out, toweling his hair, his mouth set in a grim line, Christine mustered up the strength to reassure him. "I'm going to stay in bed and get a little extra sleep," she said. She even made up a story about a friend from the office who had been afflicted by the same symptoms. "It's just the flu, really. I'll be fine by tomorrow. The best way for you to help me is to get the children off to school."

Christine saw from the look in his eyes that Ron knew there was more to the story than she was telling but was tired of being pushed away. And the children did need to get to school. And she didn't' t look to be in grave danger. He kissed the top of her forehead and whispered, "Okay. Get well soon."

Once Ron had shut the door, Christine began to cry. What a mess! Every time she closed her eyes, she felt she was back in that plane: lost in the dark, rocked and jostled by mysterious and uncaring forces, falling through space.

Then the bedroom door opened again. She brushed the tears from her eyes hurriedly and saw Ron, standing frozen in the doorway, with their neighbor June peeking out from behind him. June had been their neighbor since they had moved into their home ten years before, and she and her family had lived on the street for a long time before that. That first morning in their new home, June had brought over a plate of freshly baked fudge brownies and told them that if they ever needed any help, she would be glad to provide it. "I call myself the street mother," she told them, as she handed them the plate of treats.

In many ways she was. She and her husband, Sam, had raised their children in the house next door and grown old there. Sam had died in his sleep the winter before.

Christine didn't have time to recover and hide her red, wet face. Ron broke out of his shock and rushed to the edge of the bed, not knowing what to do. Christine saw for the first time that Ron too was lost. Lost for words, lost for ideas, lost in the awareness that he had missed a great deal of what was happening to her.

June also sensed his helplessness. "Now Ron, off you go — we'll be fine here. I'll call you in an hour and give you an update." But Ron needed some coaxing. He got only as far as the bedroom door before he turned back. Christine felt overwhelmed with pity for her husband. She mustered up just enough of a smile to give him permission to go.

June repeated, "I promise I'll call you within the hour."

As soon as Ron had left the room, Christine sat up in bed, smoothed her hair down, and began to explain. She recited the story she had told Ron earlier — the co-worker with the flu, the very same symptoms.

June sat and listened. Then she said, quietly "And what's the rest of the story?"

∘ EPIPHANY OF DESPAIR ∘

This was enough to send Christine over the edge. Tears started streaming back down her cheeks. June sat next to her on the bed, a look of sympathy on her lined face. Between the sobs, Christine tried to speak. "I don't know — I don't know what's wrong with me."

June moved a little closer and put a hand on Christine's trembling shoulder. "Well, we have all day to figure it out, so let's just sit here for a while and see what happens, all right?" She made no effort to quiet Christine down. She made it very clear she wasn't afraid of her tears.

Christine leaned against the headboard. The room was still spinning. She closed her eyes to get some relief, and then quickly opened them again. She tried to explain to June what happened whenever she closed her eyes: how the plane, the people screaming, and fear would all come rushing back. How it seemed she'd never even left the plane.

"I guess you thought you were going to die," June said. "What a horrible thing to suffer through."

Christine leaned over and melted into June's arms like a small child. She wanted to curl up in that motherly embrace and stay there for a hundred years.

June held her and stroked her hair. "You poor girl," she said, and then, very quietly, she began to sing the lyrics to "Amazing Grace." When she reached the line, "The hour I first believed," she lifted Christine's chin and looked her straight in the eyes. June repeated the words, "The hour I first believed." Now they wept together.

∘ ACCEPTANCE ∘

Christine had heard "Amazing Grace" sung many times before. She had always enjoyed the tune, but hadn't really listened to the words. "The hour I first believed … in God?" she asked.

"They sang that song at my mother's funeral," June said. "It had been her favorite. She used to sing it around the house, just making dinner or getting ready to go out. At the end of the service, when they started to sing, I knew everything in my life had changed. For the first time, I believed I would really die some day. I suppose I had thought about it before that, but I had never truly believed it. And then the choir sang the words, 'The hour I first believed.' I knew I would carry that hour with me for the rest of my life. The hour I believed that death is real. The hour I came to know the pain of accepting death as a real part of life. That was the hour I first believed."

Their tears took on a different quality now. They no longer belonged just to Christine. Nor did they belong just to June. They were the tears of everyone who had visited that cave, alone and in the dark. Both women were silent for a while.

"Oh my God, June," Christine said. "I did think I was going to die. I tried to convince myself I wouldn't, but I could have. And Charlotte and Tommy could be taking a plane and the same thing could happen to them."

June added, "Or they could be at school and something else could happen to them."

"What would I ever do without them? What would they ever do without me? What do I do now?" Christine whispered.

June's voice resumed its maternal tone. "Well, there's no doubt there's a lot of learning to be done here. But there are lots of us to help."

· ACQUIRING RESOURCES — SELF, OTHERS, GOD ·

Christine now understood that she had been awakened to the reality of death that day on the plane. To pretend otherwise would no longer be possible for her.

It was finally clear to her that she could never again pretend that death was not part of her. She could never again believe in the illusion that she could control life. She was finally awake to understanding that the awareness of death had changed the way she thought and that she would have to develop new skills to deal with what she now knew. She did not yet know what that meant, but she could see that June had somehow learned something powerful enough to make her the kind and gentle person she was. She hoped she would grow old like June and have no regrets about the life she had lived.

She was still scared. But now that she had a plan, and some of June's wisdom, she felt more prepared to take on the project.

At noon Ron came home to check on his wife. He was tentative as he walked into the room. He was happy to see Christine sitting up; even happier when she extended her arms to him.

June smiled, first at Christine and then at Ron. Then she was off, leaving Ron alone with his wife.

Ron walked over and knelt beside the bed.

Christine began to stroke his head with the same tenderness June had shown her. She understood now why Ron hadn't been able to help her. He didn't know what she knew. She thought about telling him and then she thought better. Instead, she prayed that she would be patient enough to let him learn the truth in his time and in his own way. Until then, she would hug him a little tighter and enjoy life with their children more fully.

INTERGENERATIONAL WISDOM

Don's Story

For many years I counseled older adults. With the help of their loved ones, we talked to them about what they should be eating, which medications they should be taking, and how much exercise they should be getting: all well-intentioned advice focused on showing them how to stay healthy.

Because I did not fully understand the relevance of death in healthy living, there was no communication about the topic.

It was not until my own health crisis that I began to see just how many opportunities had been missed. Death is a very relevant topic to older adults. While most have some level of anxiety about death, they may also carry a great deal of wisdom on the subject. We need to learn to interact with them more openly about death.

I missed my opportunity to learn from them, and they missed the opportunity to be helpful.

The Grief Reconciliation Process gives us a language with which to communicate.

Don's story describes how an older adult can act as a role model to us as we learn about death as part of life.

Don and his wife, Betty, arrived at the hospital early in the morning and followed the signs to the Outpatient Cardiac Clinical Investigation Unit. Neither spoke. Once they got to the unit, Don pulled out his hospital card and set it down on the counter before the nurse got a chance to ask for it. He continued to be a step ahead of her as she asked him a series of questions: Age? Seventy-six. Height? Five feet ten. Weight? One hundred sixty-eight pounds. The nurse smiled and commented that he looked much younger than his age. "Clearly you must work out," she said. Don nodded. He prided himself on the shape he was in.

As they sat in the waiting room, Betty could see tension and anxiety on Don's face. She commented on the new flat-screen television hanging from the ceiling and suggested they try to catch the morning news. When that didn't work, she offered him a magazine, noting that it was the current issue of *Sports Illustrated*. She chattered on about the chairs and their extra padding and how the waiting room looked like an airport lounge. But Don couldn't get away from the memories. The sounds coming over the crackly loudspeaker and the hospital smell had not changed one bit since he had been a patient some fifty years earlier.

Betty knew that Don's tension in hospitals dated back to when he was a middleweight boxing champion. She had seen that anxiety play itself out when their three children were born. As joyful as Don was with the birth of each of their children, he'd had a terrible time even holding the babies in the hospital. With the first birth, Betty worried he might be one of those disengaged fathers, but the minute he got baby Blake and her out of the hospital, he was as tender and involved as she ever could have dreamed.

Don was also thinking back to his boxing days. He had had his fill of the medical profession and everything that came with it. His last hospital stay was irrevocably linked in his mind with his last professional boxing match. During the fight, he had taken a direct blow to the middle of his chest: a right-hand lead. It had stunned him, but he was so sure he could take the guy that he convinced his trainer to let him continue. After going another full four rounds, the fight ended with a TKO in Don's favor.

Don was pretty cocky about having made the right call. There was a lot of hard drinking and partying that night to celebrate the big win. By the time morning rolled around, Don was in a hazy state. The booze was wearing off, his adrenaline was subsiding, and he was beginning to suspect he might be hurt. By midday, when he couldn't catch his breath, he checked himself in to the emergency department at the local hospital.

All hell broke loose. X-rays confirmed that two ribs on the left side of his chest cavity had been fractured. Both had pulled away from his sternum. The danger was that the bones could in fact puncture his lungs or heart or both. As the weeks went by, Don slowly realized that what he had was a career-ending problem, the kind that was not going to go away with time or more training.

It had taken years and a lot of help from Betty for Don to get over the devastation of leaving behind the life he loved. But he had made it, becoming the kind of man he wanted to be: hard-working, steady, a good provider to his family.

A few weeks earlier, Don had been golfing with his three closest buddies when he developed a sudden pain in his chest. It wasn't severe, just something he couldn't quite shake. At first he thought it was a bout of indigestion, but after he barely made contact with the ball when teeing off, he mentioned the discomfort to his friends. Collectively they counseled him to take it seriously. He finished the game and agreed to stop at his doctor's office on the way home, though by then the pain had all but disappeared.

The doctor had taken the visit far more seriously than Don would have liked. Don had expected him to confirm that the beer and pizza he'd had for lunch was probably not one of his better ideas. Instead, the doctor said, "We must rule out the possibility that you are having a little trouble with your heart." Then he proceeded to ask Don a whole series of questions that got him thinking. Don began to consider that maybe the pain in his chest had been around for a while. He thought back to a few weeks before. A stabbing pain in his neck when helping his son, Sam, move some furniture, had been enough to make him stop to catch his breath. Then there was the time just a few days ago when he got a cramp in his left arm while he and Betty were out for a walk. The doctor continued with the examination and recommended more tests.

Over the next few days, Don had been back and forth to the clinic for a stress test, echocardiogram, and electrocardiogram, all of which helped the doctor confirm that the pain in his chest was angina. The doctor had explained that angina is associated with high-grade narrowing of the heart arteries. The doctor had recommended that Don begin the use of nitroglycerine to treat his chest pain and ordered him to consult a cardiologist immediately. The cardiologist's office scheduled the tests at the hospital for the following day. The speed at which they made the appointment was unnerving to Don.

Finally, Don was called in for his procedure. Betty reached over and took his hand, giving it a little rub. He stood up, gave her a kiss, and said he would see her in a few hours.

The cardiologist was going to do an angiogram with possible angioplasty, a test with "some potential risks," they said, but one that was conducted routinely when anyone showed any signs of cardiac distress. The earlier tests he had undergone confirmed a diagnosis of coronary artery disease but had not given them all the answers they needed for determining how to treat him.

Don understood this procedure. Several of his friends had had one. It had helped two of them avoid cardiac bypass surgery. Angioplasty was a day procedure followed by a few days of limited activity. It was not that big a deal. The thought of being in the hospital bothered him far more than the procedure itself.

The doctors gave him general anesthetic and injected dye into his arteries. Then they threaded a long, narrow, hollow plastic tube into the blood vessel of Don's left groin until it reached the chamber of his heart. As they suspected, fatty material, plaque, had narrowed the blood vessels of his heart. They performed an angioplasty to open the coronary arteries that supply the heart muscles. In this procedure, a balloon is inflated inside a blood vessel to flatten any plaque obstructing it.

As Don came out of the anesthetic, thoughts of the old days weighed heavily on his mind. He could feel a gust of cold air in his nostrils. He tried to swallow to clear the terrible taste he had in his mouth. His throat felt as though it had been shredded by a cheese grater. He moaned with the discomfort. Then he heard his name being called: "Mr. McLean, you are in the recovery room at the General Hospital; your tests are over. Mr. McLean, it is time to wake up. Open your eyes."

Don tried to comply. His eyes were prepared to see, but his eyelids would not open. Again he drifted back to his days in the ring. He was down for the count and couldn't get up off the mat. Two ... Three ... Four ... The nurse called his name again. "Mr. McLean, Don, I need you to open your eyes." He sighed in an attempt to show her that he was trying to do what she asked. He could see the light shining through his lids. He tried again to open them. This time they flickered. Then he needed to rest. Five ... Six ... Seven ... The nurse patted his hands, insisting he try again.

Finally he got his eyes open and tried to sit up. After that, it did not take long to get back to the real world. If anything, they had to hold him back. He was a fighter. He refused the pain medication they offered him and insisted they take the tubes out of his arms. The nurse laughed. "I might have to keep you here all day if you don't slow down a bit," she said. She described how he would need to rest with his body flat as they observed him for several hours. When he was just about ready to go home, the doctor would be in to discuss the test results.

Once Don understood how the next few hours would go, he followed through.

At 2 p.m., the cardiologist appeared. By then Don was sitting on the side of his bed with his clothes beside him. The nurse laughed at his impatience. "He can't seem to get away from us fast enough," she said.

Don glanced over at the doctor. He had a serious look on his face. Typical of these guys who work too hard, he thought.

The doctor examined the small stab wound in Don's leg and then listened to his heart. He didn't look into Don's eyes. Instead, he turned away and ordered the nurse to remove the intravenous line. He told Don to get dressed and then come to his office down the hall. That was odd, Don thought. All the other surgeons were talking to their patients right there in the recovery room. Don figured this guy was particularly uptight; it was probably how he insisted on doing things.

The nurse called Betty in to help get Don into his clothes. He scoffed at them and dressed himself — a little slower than normal, but without the women's help, thank you very much. He asked Betty to wait in the waiting room and proceeded unaided down the hall to the doctor's office.

The doctor greeted him almost too warmly. Don began to think something wasn't right. What he expected the cardiologist to say was that they had cleared the affected blood vessels and he would be as good as new. What the doctor actually said was, "We were not able to remove the plaque that has formed in your vessels the way we had hoped."

Don was deeply disappointed but skipped ahead of the doctor, saying, "So does that mean cardiac bypass surgery is the next option?"

The doctor explained that surgery was always a risk in older adults. There could be a longer hospital stay and more complications. Don wasn't really listening. He didn't think of himself as an older adult. He had quit smoking thirty years ago and no longer used alcohol. He exercised daily and had the frame of a much younger man. Sure he used to be a hard-living guy, but that was many years ago. Except for a little shortness of breath, he was in excellent health.

The doctor continued his attempt to deliver the news. When he saw that Don wasn't taking anything in, he launched into an explanation of the technical issues that made surgery especially troublesome.

"The fractures to your ribs and sternum sustained years ago have created scar tissue that has complicated matters," he said. "The scar tissue behind your sternum means it would be very difficult to get at your heart because this major artery lies right behind the sternum and could easily be compromised when opening the chest."

As the doctor spoke, Don worked to stay within himself, to check out what he was up against and then make a decision on how best to handle things after he had all of the information. Bob and weave, bob and weave, he thought. No use getting too worked up yet. He shifted around in his seat, anticipating an incoming jab. When it came, it landed with more of a sting than he ever could have imagined.

"I've already consulted with two of my colleagues," the doctor was saying. "I had them come in while we were doing the procedure. You are welcome to talk to them or get someone from the outside to review your case. I am happy to help you with anything I can. But it is important that you know this, Don. The bottom line, from our perspective, is that given the circumstances, we cannot completely fix the arteries and we cannot do surgery. Your only viable option is to work to prolong your life through ongoing drug therapy."

∘ SURVIVING ∘

The doctor couldn't tell whether Don had heard him, so he repeated himself. "Don, you are not a candidate for coronary bypass surgery. While there's no way to reverse damage to your heart, treatments can significantly stabilize signs and symptoms." The doctor was now in sell mode. "The medicines we have today are helping some people to continue to live for a number of years. On your end, you can continue to exercise and stay on a good diet to help your weakened heart work as efficiently as possible."

Don could hear the shift in his voice. He knew what he was really saying was, "We cannot fix you. The drug treatments only help some people. You will deteriorate."

Pain was something Don knew intimately. Pain was a constant

reminder of his dedication to his chosen profession. An acknowledgment of the inevitable outcome of his choices. A reminder that he had always pursued his dreams. The badge of honor worn by all professional athletes.

But the pain he was feeling now was different. It was accompanied by a new sensation: fear. It was insidious. It was more difficult to grasp. "We cannot fix you" was the most painful blow he had ever taken.

Don sat there waiting for the doctor to tell him there were other options to consider. Perhaps something riskier, or experimental. Instead, silence. When the nurse opened the door to announce that the next patient was waiting, Don felt the weight of defeat. He realized that the bell had rung; the fight was over. He would have to get himself up and out of the ring.

When he walked back to the waiting room, Betty hopped out of her chair and met him halfway. He didn't look at her but just barked, "Get me the hell out of here." Betty did not try to ask. She knew better.

On the trip home, Don found himself staring silently out of the window, alternating between feeling numb and revisiting the worst-case scenario. Part of him ached for information, but another part did not want to know any of it. He hated the lack of control. Betty tried to ask what the doctor had to say. Don said he was too worn out to talk. Betty was annoyed at his selfish behavior but chalked it up to his love of hospitals. She would just get him home and settled and then they could talk about what was next.

But Don was no better later that day, or the next, or the next after that.

Each morning he got up and walked around the house. He didn't go to the door to get the newspaper. He didn't answer the door or return any of his calls. It seemed to his family that he was completely disengaged. He appeared to be doing nothing.

In fact, Don was doing a great deal. He was trying to survive the news he had just received. He had fought a few bouts like that, when he was getting it handed to him but good and he knew he had to survive until he got his chance. He had seen some good fighters go down in those moments, because they just did not know how to survive. As things kept coming at him, Don was thinking, if I give in here, it's all over. So instead, he became more focused. He was working to get context, trying to figure out what he was up against.

When Don was younger and came up against a particularly difficult opponent, he would probe the fighter, circling him in a steady clockwise direction, exploring his strengths and weaknesses, flicking a jab and moving away: stick and slide, stick and slide. If things got bad during a fight and he was up against the ropes, he would go into a protective crouch. He would keep his hands and elbows up around his head, absorb the blows of the opponent, and feel his strength ebb and flow. During those moments, he and his nemesis were the only two people on the earth, existing only through and for each other.

During the days after the body blow he had received at the hospital, nothing seemed real to him. He was managing the news the way he always had. The only thing he knew how to do was fight. His defensive stance did not allow anyone to get too close. He refused to talk to anyone, including his wife. Occasionally he would think he should, but then he would think about the energy that would take. What would he say? How would he begin? He knew how she would begin. She would ask him how he was feeling, and then she would be annoyed when he told her he felt nothing. The truth was that he felt both nothing and everything at the same time. One foot on the gas, the other on the brake. He was facing the specter of a long slow deterioration, raging against the passage of time.

Don tried to slow his mind down so he could see his options clearly. He spent hours and hours trying to figure out a way to set a different strategy. He was fighting with himself and with the news. On the one hand, he was thinking there must be some way out of this mess; on the other hand, he was trying not to think about it at all. He knew he was in crisis but had no idea which approach to take. A bypass he could understand. It was real, physical. He could recover from it and go back to being strong again. But growing old, deteriorating, becoming feeble, becoming dependent on others was more than a former boxer could take. That's why he didn't know what to say when his family asked him what was going on.

His mind drifted back to the times he would sit in the dressing room preparing to be summoned into the ring. There was no talking. He was absolutely focused on the task before him, his inner voice reciting the cadence of his sequences. Nothing could distract him in those moments. He was gearing up, getting ready to engage, tolerating only optimistic thoughts. When the bell rang, the crowd roared and his adrenaline would surge.

Don tried to get back to that place: he would harness his thoughts and use all of his resources to banish the fear, anger, and sadness he could feel rising up.

The children checked in with Betty to see how Don's tests had gone, and Don refused to talk to them. That's when Betty knew the situation was serious. Don could on occasion distance himself from her, but he never turned away from his children.

The children did their best to break through the tension, but Don made it increasingly difficult for them. His daughter Jenna came over to visit him one day and when he mentioned he had an upset stomach, she went to the fridge and started throwing out all the food. Don accused her of thinking they were too stupid to know how to feed themselves and told her to stop trying to take over their lives. She left in tears.

A week after Don's cardiac procedure, their middle child, Sam, tried a different approach. He came over on a Sunday afternoon, on the pretense of wanting to discuss his future at work. Don understood what was going on. Sam was there to get him to talk. He was there to find out how he felt. The truth was that Don did not know how he felt. He had never been in this type of situation before. How did he feel at this moment? How did he feel about the news he had just received that they weren't able to operate? He had no idea. He did not yet know what it all meant. He had opened his eyes that morning and he was still here. So what did it mean?

After a few pleasantries, Sam posed the question. It wasn't really a question. It was a statement, maybe even a demand for answers.

"Dad, I want you to tell me what the doctor told you the other day," he said.

Don's eyes narrowed. He stood perfectly still, not one hair moving, breathing slow and deep. When Don refused to talk about his health, the fight was on. Don claimed his health was no one's business. Sam called him "a stubborn old man." As they went back and forth, they began to yell at each other. Don slammed a cupboard door as a warning, and Sam knocked the papers off the kitchen table to defy him.

When Don raised his fist, Sam took a step toward his dad and asked, "What the hell do you think you're doing?" As he looked at his father, he remembered how when he was a teenager the two of them had stood in that very kitchen and come to blows. It was on that day that Sam had learned how irrevocably linked they were, neither able to win because in winning they would both lose.

His father was big, strong, and clearly able to force his point of view. Sam was a scared teenager, desperately trying to be a man. Instead of allowing the fight to get beyond them, his father had taken control. He had opened his fists and exposed the palms of his hands, and then extended his arms. Without saying another word, he had taken a series of very slow steps toward Sam. Sam had used angry words to hold his father back, but his dad had slowly wrapped his arms around him and said, "Son, I love you."

In that moment and forever, they were one. Sam could no longer keep his father out. In that moment, his father had shown him how to back down; how to let someone you love save face; how to be a man.

Now, as Sam studied his aging father's face, he could see the fear in his father's eyes. It scared Sam to see the strength of such a strong man slipping away. He approached his dad the way he had been taught. He opened his arms and invited him into his embrace. The hostility ended the same way it had ended all those years before. They both let down and felt each other's embrace.

Sam was so consumed by the thought of his father being frail that he could not say what he wanted to say, which was, "Dad, I love you, and I'm going to help you deal with whatever's going on."

Don, so unaccustomed to being weak, was equally at a loss. He wanted to say, "I'm scared. I am afraid to be dependent on my family. I want to go down like a man," but he could not get the words out.

So neither spoke. Both wanting to ask; both afraid to know. Instead, they held each other for a few moments longer. The arguing had not resolved the issues, but it had broken the tension. Though neither realized it, it had set the stage for them to start moving forward.

It was hard for Don to let his wife see him this way. He pulled away from his son the moment he heard her voice. Sam let go of his dad and walked over to greet his mom. Betty was relieved to see that the fighting was over.

That night, while Don and Betty lay in bed, Betty tried again to ask him what the doctor had said. "I want to know, Don," she said. "I really want to know."

But as soon as Don tried to tell her, her eyes filled with tears. Don did not know how to take care of her, how to protect her from being hurt by the news, so he summarized the facts about the surgery and assured her that the medication they had prescribed was just as good. He reached over and gave her a hug and said they ought to get some sleep.

Over the next few days, Betty coped the only way she knew how. She would tell him things were going to be fine. During the day, when the sun was shining, he could almost believe her, but at night he would find himself awake and alone, realizing that he was dying and that no one would let him talk about it.

Apart from Sam and Betty, the rest of his family had their own issues. They could not bear the thought of thinking about death, so they did what they could to take back control. They rode in on their high horses, driven to find answers. It was as though they thought the whole thing was simply a misunderstanding, that if the correct information could be obtained, the problem would go away. When Don tried to question their actions, they argued that he was more frightened than informed. He agreed to more tests, more for them than for himself.

· ASSESSING — SELF, OTHERS, GOD ·

In his heart, Don knew the outcome would be the same. He had seen the scans and read the test results. He knew the facts about his condition. He believed his doctor had tried everything and that nothing else could be done. So having the news of his cardiac condition confirmed did not surprise him to the same extent that it upset the rest of the family.

As distressing as the news was for the family to hear, Don felt he did not have the energy to take care of them. He was dealing with his own issues. He developed a bothersome obsession with his health, believing every symptom to spell the end. A cold came to mean pneumonia: death. A pain in his back came to mean a cardiac arrest: death. He would have to talk to himself and harness his thoughts. He would have to fight to get out from under the fear. The effort it took was extraordinary and left him no energy for anything else. He could not help his family. He knew he could break down at any minute.

It was an emotional time. In order not to get knocked off his feet, he talked about sports and the stock market and stayed away from anyone who might drag him down. He was angry, and his family was in hyper-gear. No one knew what to do. Each suffered, alone.

∘ DEPRESSION ∘

In his youth, Don had been the essence of physical skill, strength, and grace. To be physically diminished was to be an object of pity. The thought of it was unbearable to him.

He had always believed in absolute preparation, but this time the question was, prepared for what? The ambiguity of the whole situation tortured him. No game plan that he had mapped out, no amount of training had prepared him to face this opponent whose strength was as overwhelming as the tide.

His present nemesis was of a different kind: invisible but powerful enough to put him down for the count. The more he tried to control his thoughts of death, the more death threatened him. For the first time he was looking into the face of an opponent he had no weapons to defend himself against. No amount of training seemed to have prepared him. Just like his toughest moments in the ring, he could feel his strength leaving him. Although his will remained strong, he feared that this time he was fighting an enemy who was more determined, more resolute.

Whom could he turn to? How would he train? How could he face up to his greatest fear, of being a frail old man waiting to die?

In his mind he was confused between the concept of letting nature take its course and euthanasia. Medicine and technology would have one believe there was a solution to everything. And that if a solution could not be found, then someone had missed something or the patient had done something wrong. That whole attitude created fear and denial, and left him feeling a failure.

On one hand, he had his family telling him it was his duty to fight death. On the other hand, he was trying to get used to the idea that he might not have what it would take to fight this one. It was very confusing. Everyone wanted him to take action, but no one was able to talk about what was really going on.

He woke up every morning and someone else would tell him he ought to be going somewhere to get a third, fourth, fifth opinion, that he should fly here or there, that he should not believe what he was being told about the test results. The implication was that if he did not pursue these leads, he was giving in to killing himself. Part of him wanted to believe they were right, that he ought to rage against death. But a small inner voice was starting to say, just settle down — you are seventy-six, after all. Do you actually think you're going to live forever? But then he wondered, do I just let nature take its course, or do I gear up and go to battle with this thing?

Back and forth, back and forth he would go all day and often into the night. It was very hard to get sound advice from anyone: the doctor was assuring him that the drugs he was taking would help keep him alive; the family was telling him to keep fighting for their sake.

Don began to see what a socially private issue death is. People could talk about dying in the abstract, they could talk about a friend who died, but they would not talk about death as it related to them. They would not say how they felt about the reality of it, the inevitability of it, how they prepared for it or learned to live with the reality of it. He could see how extremely hesitant everyone around him was to accept death as a part of living. It was as though everyone felt that talking about death as real would make death happen.

Don was confused. Everyone wanted him to reject death at all costs. They were all ears for that. But talk about death quietly and reasonably and they said, "Shhh! Enough of that. Everything's going to be all right." He was struck by the irony of having to pretend he was fine in order to support those around him who could not handle the truth that he might soon be dead. All the more reason not to talk about any of this.

He wondered whether anyone knew what was going on. He knew many people who read the obituaries every morning. They must have a realistic understanding of what can go wrong with their bodies, he thought, and yet they still seemed to be left on their own to make sense of it. Did people not know they were all moving closer to death? Did his family think he could not see what was happening to his friends? Did they not think he knew that we are built to self-destruct? How stupid did everyone think he was?

The thought of death would come to him and he would try to tackle it. But it was hard to fight. It was hard not to fight. It was hard to know how to fight. It was just plain hard.

Don could see this wasn't just his conflict. He could see that even the churches had gone into the business of promoting the illusion that if one prayed, the burden of suffering could be lifted. It was as though everyone had forgotten there is a bottom line and that one day it would all end. Don went to church with his wife. While she prayed, he had his own conversation with God: Is this what some Christians call purgatory? I'm not dead but I'm not really alive. I'm not winning, but I'm not down for the count yet, either.

In the quiet hours of the morning, usually between 2 and 4 a.m., Don often found himself trying to pull the pieces together: He was ill. He was going to die. He was afraid of death. He was afraid of dying. He was afraid of not dying like a man.

In his younger days, when sitting around after a fight, late at night, he and his buddies would talk about fighting until the end — going out in a blaze of glory. Nowhere in that scenario was it written that you should die old, frail, dependent, and pitied by those around you.

He wished he could speak to his family with his heart, but how? The words would not come; the language was always just beyond his grasp.

It was during one of those early mornings that Don's mind started to go farther and farther back to his early years.

· Epiphany of Despair ·

Don thought of when he was a boy. He thought about his older sister, Stella, and wondered how he knew she was dying. Had anyone told him? Had he figured it out on his own? Had they used words to talk about it? How did Stella live for all of those years knowing? He was sure she knew. They used to talk openly about it.

When Don was fourteen, Stella, four years his senior, died a slow death in the family home. Stella's "weak heart" had made her frail for many years before that. In fact, Don wasn't sure there was ever a time when she was strong enough to do chores. That did not preclude her from taking an active role in family life. He remembered her as a beautiful smile always home to receive them. Don hadn't thought about Stella for many years; some of the memories were too painful. Particularly the memory of the day she died.

Late one summer afternoon, while he was sitting with Stella, she reached over, gently took his hand, and looked into his eyes with a hauntingly passionate look. Then she asked him to go get Mother. Don ran right away to get her. They had never been told that Stella would get well, or that they ought to pretend she was just sick and not dying, so when he saw the look on her face, he understood what was about to happen.

His mother went into the room, talked to Stella for a few minutes, and then came out with her eyes full of tears, whispering, "Go and find your father."

Don did not dare ask where he was. He set out on foot to search the many fields.

When he finally did find his dad, he was cutting up some timber down at the mill. Don had been so intent on his search he hadn't thought of what he would say. He stood completely out of breath waiting for the right words to come. He was hoping his father would guess, so he wouldn't have to say anything. His father did not want to guess, and Don did not want to find the right words. Somehow Don mustered up the strength to deliver the message. His father, upon receiving the news, was so grief-stricken he hopped on his horse and galloped off without a word.

When Don thought about Stella, all he remembered was that moment of standing by himself, a young boy, who had mustered up the courage to be the kind of man his mother wanted him to be, only to be abandoned, left in a field alone, watching his father ride off to join his mother and his dying sister.

For years he had internalized that moment and reacted to it. It had covered up the wonderfully powerful feelings he had for his sister. It had created a terrible rift between him and his father.

It was that rage that had taken him to the boxing ring.

Now, as he thought more about death and being with death, he could see there was more to it than just the day Stella died. He thought about Stella — what it felt like to be with her; the kind of life she had even though she knew she was dying — and realized that there must have many more moments before the moment when she died.

When Don thought about himself as a boy, he did not remember feeling sad around Stella. He was always happy to be with her. She was always happy to be with him. He loved coming home from school to sit with her. She was the one who helped him sort out his problems. They would discuss life together, always in an equal exchange. He would bring her news of the outside world; she would help him see there was another dimension to life. Don often wondered whether she was the one who lived in the real world, with the rest of them just playing some kind of game.

Despite her physical frailty, Stella was spiritually stronger and more grounded than anyone he knew. She talked openly about death as if it was the most natural part of life. They would discuss God. She would wonder about his plan for her. She would say she didn't know for sure what awaited her on the other side of life, but she didn't worry too much about that. Her willingness to move forward in faith despite her doubts exemplified to all those who came into contact with her a true wisdom and humility, one that offered hope.

Odd, now that Don thought about it, because she never actually went anywhere or did anything. Yet she could make them all feel both very settled and highly energized. Don delighted in hearing her soften the arrogant stance of those she came into contact with. He delighted in hearing her make their father laugh. It was those wonderful moments that Don missed. Yes, Stella's dying had put an end to the moments, but the fact that she lived for many years knowing death would come had not harmed them. How they handled her death, how they turned away from each other as they suffered: that had done the family a great deal of harm.

As Don thought about Stella, he remembered that he was not sad to be in the presence of death. He was sad to be without the presence of death. He was sad when she was gone, sad that he could no longer be with her. The fact that she was not strong enough to live forever had not precluded her from playing an extremely important role in their family. Stella was the one everyone went to when they had news to share. She was the one everyone confided in, the one who helped them set strategy and attack the world. She lived her life that way: challenging them to see the difference between the artificial life that masks the true meaning of life and the authentic life that allows death to be real.

Stella did not simply survive her life. She lived it. The memory of her courage was calling him now. Calling him to sit with the news he had received a few weeks before. Calling him to handle the news the way she had: by simply honoring the truth to reconcile it, and in doing so to live each day he had left to the fullest.

Many years ago, he had stopped talking about Stella. Her memories were too precious to share. Now he could see that by locking her memory away, he had missed the essence of her. He had not discussed her much with his children. He had not discussed with them that even in her frail state, she had added great value to his life. No wonder his family was afraid of death. They had no experience of it.

∘ ACCEPTANCE ∘

For the first time in many years, he could hear his sister's voice again, calling him in to have a chat. He found himself asking how she stayed engaged with those she loved. How she found the strength to be honest and open in the face of death. How she lived knowing she did not have much time.

Don couldn't understand how Stella kept from counting the hours she had left. She did not count how many people came to see her, or how fair life was. Instead, she lived. She cherished the moments she had with her family. She cherished the opportunities she had to connect with people. She cherished life. Don could see that all he had been doing since getting the news from the doctors was counting. The counting had completely paralyzed him. The counting was standing in the way of his being able to live.

Don began to see that he was more afraid of being afraid than he was of death. His family, too, was afraid of being afraid. They were afraid they could not bear to see their father weak; afraid they would not know how to spare him the burden of suffering; afraid they would not know the right thing to say, the right things to do. It was his fears about his children's fears and their fears about their parents' fears that made it difficult for them to talk about death. It was not death itself. They were all focused on the fear of having to manage the moment when he might be dead.

Don could see the difference now. They were focused on the dying and not on the living getting ready to die. He would always be afraid of dying, but that did not mean he would have to be afraid of living. Like his sister, he would not close his eyes and pretend that death was not real. Nor would he hand himself over to death. In Stella's memory, he would train himself to walk in harmony with death.

As he got back in touch with his memories of Stella, Don came to see the split between the outside world that masks the true meaning of life and makes one fear death, and the authentic life that puts death onto a real plane in proper context with life.

He realized that he was not fighting death. He had been fighting the temptation to close his eyes or turn his back on his family. He was fighting the temptation to disengage because he was afraid to stay awake for fear of what he might see; he was afraid of the suffering he might cause. But Don knew in his heart that Stella had not lived that way. She had stood her ground like a true fighter. She had prepared for the day she would meet death. So Don got to work on the things that needed to be done. He began to prepare for the biggest bout of his life.

He began to think about ways he could tackle his fears. He began to think strategically about what he could do to help himself and his family. He did not wish to leave his wonderful Betty and his three children standing alone in a field, trying to make sense of things themselves. He loved them too much. He wanted them to know how dependent they were on each other. He wanted them to know about the major gaps that are left to be filled when a loved one leaves.

He made a commitment to reach out to his family as his learning began. He would start by trying to explain what he was going through. He would have to learn how to develop the language to speak of it. That didn't mean they would need to sit around and talk about death to the exclusion of other things. It just meant that they ought not to pretend it wasn't going to happen. When the day did finally come for Don to die, his family might well be upset and distressed, but death would not be a shock that would make them turn away from each other.

Accepting that death is real did not mean he was giving up. He was simply accepting that he had to learn how to live with the uncertainty that faced him. He knew where he was; he did not know where he was going.

° ACQUIRING RESOURCES — SELF, OTHERS, GOD °

As Don began to think about death differently, it occurred to him that he had a lot of work to do. His family did not know how to support him because they had not had the opportunity to learn. Because he had been so physically strong — because he could harness his emotions and focus so intently on the task at hand — he was the one they counted on. Don realized that in wanting to protect them, he had not taught them what they might need to know. He understood that no one volunteered to learn about death. But that was the point. The day had come when they did not have a choice and he would have to be strong enough to teach them.

Don's challenge was to convey his wisdom to those he loved. He called his family together and reviewed what the doctor had told him about not being able to operate. He also explained in extremely emotional terms what he was feeling and why. He was not smooth in his explanation, but he was clear, and his family instantly felt a great burden had been lifted off them. He explained that there were things to be taken care of. There were important decisions to be made, business documents that must be discussed and signed: his estate-planning portfolio, with both a living will and a last will. There were decisions to be made about his burial and funeral arrangements, including how the bills would be paid.

Don explained that getting these things out of the way would give him peace of mind that his Betty would be well cared for after he was gone. That helped his children, but only a little. It was a difficult conversation. A sad conversation with a lot of tears. But it was a conversation that they had together. As a family. Not a conversation they would have to have alone after he was gone.

With time Don learned to articulate what was happening, and his children began to find ways to be helpful. The next time Sam asked how he felt about his recent doctor's appointment, Don responded, "Funny enough, I am not as scared about death as I used to be when I was young. It's like I am passed the expiry date and still going, so I guess that's okay." His son could ask, and he could speak. Once Don came to see death as real, it relaxed him a bit. He said to Betty, "Oh hell, this is what it is, so why fight it?" Betty could see him getting more contemplative and less agitated.

Over the next months Don began to see that there were some advantages to having learned to dance with death. He understood how little peace there was in the outside world, with everyone so busy counting. Counting physical strength and beauty; counting how much money one had or did not have; counting who owes what; counting everything, all the time. The sharper the mind, the greater the inclination to keep score. Don could see the importance of counting, but he no longer wanted to get caught up in it. Counting only served to confuse him. If he only had a short time left, did it matter how much more or less time he had than someone else?

Occasionally, Don would find himself looking back at his life and looking ahead at the life of his children with him out of the picture. He was torn between wanting to prepare them to be without him and wanting to demand that they stay close to him. Then he would find himself counting again, and he would tell himself to stop, just be.

He talked to God and sometimes he could hear a quiet voice deep inside him telling him that no matter what happened, things would somehow be okay. He was no longer afraid of what the future held. Was that faith? He didn't know. He did know that it gave him great comfort. It was like the voice of the dear friend who called him and said, "Don't try too hard to figure it all out. Just be. You cannot count what will be — the number of possibilities goes to infinity. Do not count how much time you have or don't have, or whether you have been loved enough. Just be."

. His memory of his sister Stella helped him to begin seeing the world differently. Instead of measuring productivity in dollars or physical strength, he was learning to count the tenderness he saw in people's eyes — the gestures of kindness shown to him by others. He learned to assess how engaged he was in all the things he was doing. He learned to ask, "Am I spending the time I have left in a meaningful way? Have I done everything necessary for me to be free to go today?"

Don began to see that the most valuable gifts he could give his children were the same ones Stella had given him: the humility and wisdom he had collected over a lifetime of hard work. Gifts that had the potential of reaping rewards long after he was gone.

By being able to rely on his family the way Stella had relied on him, he was allowing his children to be strong. As he watched them come and go; as they learned to engage with both him and Betty; as they learned to adjust to the change in circumstance they were all faced with, Don could see how strong and competent they were becoming.

By depending on his family rather than turning away from them, Don had made a choice: to let those who cared about him be with him as he as he made the transition from a strong and dominant man to a wise and insightful patriarch.

It was becoming absolutely clear to Don that he had won the biggest bout of all.

REPRESENTING THE DEAD

Rita's Story

Over the years, I have interviewed hundreds of people who are bereaved. I have learned a great deal from those who have had to learn to live with death. They are an exceptionally brave group. They learn to live when they may not want to live, seeing good in a world that has caused them extraordinary pain.

Among this group are parents who have lost children. Rita's story focuses on how a woman survived the unimaginable death of her twenty-year-old son: how she moved from being a dedicated, loving mother to a suicidal, grieving woman, and back to an open, loving human being. You will hear how she came apart; how she learned to be with suffering; and how she learned to put herself back together: a very complex puzzle that joined her present, past, and future.

~

Rita approached the stage with a great deal of trepidation. Even all these years since her son died, she wondered whether she would get through the speech she had been asked to give.

"Thank you for allowing me to speak to you today," she said. She took a moment, as she always did, to look around the room. She knew that no one came to listen to a speech about death without a good reason.

Some in the audience were clearly academics — they had their pens in hand, ready to jot down notes. Rita hoped she could add to the body of knowledge on the topic of death by articulating the process of recovery. Some were clinicians. She hoped she could impart to them an understanding of the pain and suffering involved, so they could deliver compassionate care to those in need. The rest were the ones she could most relate to. They were the walking wounded, desperate for relief: parents and loved ones who were bereaved. They were the ones who would spend the rest of their lives representing only the dead, unless she could help them learn how to represent all of their loved ones, both the living and the dead.

"It is hard to believe the direction of one's life can change so quickly, but that is what happens," she said. "You think you're living the life meant for you, and then in a fraction of a moment that life has completely changed. You try at first to think it is all a mistake, that one day you will get back to the life you were living. But you never do. You must learn to create a new way of living.

"Before that moment came for me, my family and I were living what many would describe as a charmed life. Yes, we had our little ups and downs — after all, we were married." She paused while people laughed. "We had three children." Again, laughter. "We did have our fights in the car when we were out for family bonding time. We did, on occasion, let the stress of work or lack of sleep cause us to be unkind to each other. But overall we felt loved and supported by each other. We were each enjoying a certain amount of success: the kids at school, my husband in business, and I as a reporter for a major newspaper. Before the night I received a phone call, that is.

"For the clinicians and academics in the room, I want to share with you some of what the bereaved must live through. For the rest of you, I know you have your own story that is every bit as heart-wrenching as mine. I hope I do not in any way suggest that I am better acquainted with suffering than you are. My goal is simply to share with you what I have learned."

Then, knowing that she had her listeners' full attention, Rita carried on without digression.

At 2:45 a.m. on April 8, 1954, I received a phone call. It began with, "Mrs. Montclair? This is Inspector James Gibbons of the state police calling. We are coming to your front door. We need to speak with you right away." I sat up and threw the phone down on the bed, hoping it was a dream. As I sat there in the dark, I could hear the voice on the other end of the phone: "Mrs. Montclair, is there someone there with you? Is there someone we can call to be with you?" I thought maybe it was a crank call, but something about the voice and the way he used my name made me pick up the phone. I transferred it from ear to ear in a frantic attempt to listen, but I didn't really want to hear.

Then the doorbell rang. I jumped out of bed and ran out of my room. As I got to the hallway, I could see the red flashing lights of two police cruisers parked in front of my house. I sat down on the steps. The doorbell rang again. Then came a knock. I walked down the steps to the front door. My first thought was of my husband, Marc. We had enjoyed a lovely family lunch that day, after which he had left with a group of old friends for his annual golf trip. The knock came again. I opened the door.

In front of me stood two uniformed officers. I waited for them to tell me that I had nothing to worry about; instead, they repeated my name. "Mrs. Montclair, I am Inspector James Gibbons. This is agent Louise Sanderson from the trauma unit. Is your husband home?" I heaved a sigh of relief. Clearly I was wrong. It couldn't be Marc. They wouldn't ask for him if something had happened to him.

My relief was very quickly interrupted by, "Mrs. Montclair, is there someone here with you?" In that moment, my breathing stopped. I stood very still. As I studied the faces of the two police officers, I knew something terrible had happened. I felt like a sword was slowly being forced down my throat, through my heart, right into the pit of my stomach. "Mrs. Montclair, is there someone we can call to be with you?"

I thought about my daughter, Sophie, who was asleep upstairs. And then I thought about our sons: Paul, who was on a study week road trip with his buddies, and Sam, who was at university an hour's drive away. I swallowed hard, past the pain, and pleaded with the officers, "Please tell me why you are here."

The inspector began, "Mrs. Montclair, we have reason to believe that your son, Paul, has been involved in a very serious car accident. Is there someone we can call to be with you?" I was in such distress that I grabbed his arm. I was in such pain that he knew he could not keep the truth from me any longer. I asked the question, he gave me the answer. Our twenty-year-old son was dead.

◦ SURVIVING ◦

Even all these years later, I can still describe that night in pain-staking detail. I can tell you where I was standing, what I was thinking, the color of the flowers in the living room. I can tell you how important the police were. They came in and helped make the phone call to my husband. They helped make the necessary arrangements to get him home. They helped me get in touch with the people at the university where our oldest son, Sam, was studying. They arranged for his best friend and a counselor to be with him when they told him the news. They sat with me while I told our daughter, Sophie. They stayed with me until Marc arrived home in the wee hours of the morning. I'm telling you how grateful I am to the officers, because I am certain that without someone there, I would not have been brave enough to take my next breath.

Unlike that first night, the days and weeks that followed blended together, day into night, night into day. There was no waking up in the morning and no resting at night, just a constant stream of torturous pain: the kind of pain that forced me into a semi-conscious state, begging for any kind of relief. Friends did their best to offer words of comfort, but to hear them meant I would have to open my eyes and acknowledge what was happening around me. The only way I could get through the day was to be careful not to think too much, not to see too much. As grateful as I would be later for the kind gestures, initially I had absolutely no choice but to remain partially numbed. I took the medication prescribed by the family doctor. But in the back of my mind, I knew it was a very temporary solution.

You see, I already knew death and what it can do to a family. I understood the price one pays to suffer alone. I was no stranger to pain or the destruction grief can leave in its path.

When I was a teenager, my little brother died from an accident while helping my dad with chores on our farm. In the days that followed, both of my parents went off on their own. My mother spent hours standing silently looking out the kitchen window, as though waiting for her only child to come in for dinner; my father retreated to the shed behind the house and drank. I sat by myself in the back hall, halfway between a woman who could no longer mother me and a father who had disappeared. I sat there alone, rocking back and forth with the pain.

After weeks of torture, in total desperation, I began to look for ways to escape.

I found some relief at school. One teacher in particular was exceptionally kind. Ms. Carron approached me on my first day back at school and told me I could come to her office if I needed a place to go during the day. She seemed to understand what I was going through. I never did ask her what had happened to make her know, but I could see in her eyes that she did. She told me we could talk or not talk; it was completely up to me. I took her up on her offer because I had nowhere else to go. Later, as I saw the good it was doing me, I went to absorb her compassion. The teacher and I did not have a close relationship before the trauma, but looking back I credit this woman with saving my life.

The door to her office was always open. She would look up and smile but never be the first to speak. Sometimes I would tell her about my day; sometimes we would just sit and say nothing at all. Day after day, I would sit in the office and breathe, just breathe in the air that hadn't been poisoned by grief.

What I am hoping to tell you is that sometimes it is the kindness of a virtual stranger that can have the most impact on one's life. I say this for two reasons: Don't be too quick to turn down help if you are in trouble. And, when suffering is in the air, it is everyone's business to help.

So I had an advantage when faced with the death of our son: I already knew about suffering. I knew how potent and dangerous it could be. I knew that in order to be awake one had to tolerate the pain. To numb the suffering was to be asleep. I knew I could not do to my children what had been done to me. I could not let my children suffer, abandoned by both parents. I was on the lookout for behaviors that turn grief into poison. I knew all too well what the poison could do. I had watched it slowly kill both my father and my mother. As tempting as it was, I knew I could not hide from my family. If I did, I too would abandon my living children for the one who had died.

I didn't quite know how we were going to cope, but I did know we must somehow learn to suffer together. I knew that in order to survive, we would have to learn to manage our suffering. Marc agreed that the children should stay home from school for the next while and that together we would all do our best to learn how to go on living again.

Unfortunately, my earlier experience with grief didn't mean I knew what to do; it just meant I knew what *not* to do.

· ASSESSING — SELF, OTHERS, GOD ·

We tried and tried over the next days to take care of each other, but the grief was so thick I feared it would smother us. When my good friend — our next-door neighbor — asked what she could do to help, I told her about how the teacher had helped me earlier. My friend took action. She had keys to her house made for each family member and invited each of us to come and go from her home whenever we needed. Then she asked for a key to our home. She said to me, "I think this place needs a mother."

Those words were terribly hard to hear. I wanted to scream at her and tell her to get out of my house. But she was speaking the truth. Perhaps she could have sugarcoated her statement a wee bit, but her words forced me to come face to face with the cold hard facts. Despite what I had wanted to accomplish by being available to my children, they needed more than I alone was able to give.

Over the years, I had so faulted my own mother, and now I had to admit I could barely manage my own personal care, let alone the care of those I loved. I had become utterly incompetent at managing even the simplest tasks. So when my friend offered, I knew I didn't really have a choice. If I relied on myself, I would starve my family, just as my parents had starved me.

As humbling as it was to admit it, I realized that if we were going to make it, we not only had to stay together but would also have to be brave enough to let others witness our suffering. Looking back, I am very grateful I was able to see my own limitations. I guess I have my parents to thank for that.

Further complicating things, it was proving difficult for me to be with some of our friends. I found myself trying to figure out who I could count on to be helpful. Some, whom I had considered to be good friends prior to the tragedy, were unable to help. They seemed to want to feed on the details of our son's death. They would ask odd questions, such as, "Where was he going? What time of night was it? Who called to tell you?" As if any of those questions would make him less dead. I couldn't tell if it was an awkward attempt to relate to our pain or some weird attempt to find out how they could avoid the same fate. I was already fighting those questions back myself. I was so vulnerable at the time, I did not have any energy left to take care of myself, let alone anyone else.

First thing in the morning, my neighbor would arrive, open the curtains on the main floor, and let in the light. Then she would open the windows to let some air in. After that she would make breakfast, put it on the counter, and leave, always without saying a word. In the late afternoon, she would do the same: slip in, prepare some dinner, and leave. Her gesture was saying, "I will take care of you without asking for anything in return. You do not have to suffer alone."

Slowly, Sophie and Sam began to find comfort in her presence. They would sit quietly and not say a word. Then they began to engage her in conversation. That hurt me because I wished I was strong enough to be the one they were talking to. Then they began going over to my friend's house. I encouraged them to go, but when they left, I tortured myself with self-doubt: Was I losing my children? Could I be doing more?

Through all of this, Marc did his best to be strong, but he was battling the same demons I was. He and I would sit next to each other and cry. I would slip into a deep well of sorrow. At the bottom of the well, I would lie in the darkness and plead for comfort. The deafening silence would overcome me, and the screaming for answers would start. What went wrong and why? Could this have been prevented somehow? Was there someone, anyone I could blame? Why would a God who was good allow such a thing to happen, first to my mother and now to me? Were we paying for some transgression? Was the family cursed? Is there indeed a God? If there is, why had he forsaken me in my hour of need?

There were no answers. No comfort, no insight, and no guardian angel standing next to me. There was nothing but pain and no way to make it stop.

Marc did his best to comfort me. Initially it was for his benefit that I tolerated his touch. What I didn't know at the time was that there are physiological benefits to allowing oneself to be held. Even though emotionally and psychologically one may be far away, one's body needs to be anchored. When I was in my husband's arms, my breathing would slow, and my heart would stop racing. I could begin to see the walls of the well, I could see how far down I was, and I could wonder whether I would ever see the light of day again. In his arms, I began to see the limitations of all those who offered to help. I began to question God. I concluded that there was no way to fix the problem. There was no solution. In his arms, I learned something very critical: how to accurately assess the reality of my situation. I did not have the skills to cope.

The other thing I didn't realize at the time was that by accepting help from my friend, and my husband, I was helping my children. I was showing them how to be with suffering: how to be vulnerable, how to be apart. I was teaching them how to assess their own limitations. Sophie and Sam learned how to let others hold them as they suffered through the waves of torture that washed over them during the day. They began to model what Marc and I were doing for each other by allowing us to hold them. They began to comfort us. Together we were all a little braver.

Their tenderness allowed me to open my eyes and begin to see that I had been thrown into a giant well. Without being able to see what I was up against, I might never have been able to set the systems in place to learn what had to be learned.

I did not yet know what I needed to learn, but I did know that doing nothing was not an option. I decided to get some help.

◦ DEPRESSION ◦

Six months after our son's death, I checked myself in to the psychiatry department of our local hospital. My family was very supportive. They could see I had to try something different. The staff at the hospital didn't quite know what to do with me. First of all, they were not used to people volunteering to come to the hospital. Second, they were not used to working with someone who didn't look pathetic. But just because I wore expensive clothes and was articulate did not mean I had my act together. It's true that as a reporter I was trained to keep myself in check when I had to, but that was all an illusion.

Although I was proud of the fact that I had been able to work with my family through the initial crisis, beneath the surface I was in big trouble. I would find myself thinking about death. I would fantasize about being dead. Of course, I didn't want to torture my husband and children by making it my fault, but if I could figure out a way to be lucky enough to die, that would have been great. I found myself taking ever more risks, sacrificing my personal safety in various ways. I was thinking about going back to work and volunteering to go to some geographic zone riddled with crime or drugs or war. I would find myself driving too fast when I was alone in my car. I would fantasize about going over a cliff and then I would see the face of my son.

Was I suicidal? I don't know. Did I want to join my son

wherever he was? Did I want to stop hating God and feeling so cynical about life? Did I want to stop the pain? You bet I did.

That is why I checked myself in to the hospital. I thought if I stayed at home I might just give in and that would make me even worse than my own mother. What a mess.

The staff began my treatment by helping me address the physical discomfort I was in. I had a stabbing pain that cut across my chest and ran through my heart. It came and went with every breath I took. Everything about my body felt heavy; all my energy was gone. It was hard to lift my head off my pillow in the morning. It was hard to move my legs; my feet ached. I had been in so much pain for such a long time that the natural rhythm of my body was gone. I had stiffened up and taken on robotic movements.

The hospital workers recommended a few sessions of meditation to help me get reacquainted with my body. What I learned from those sessions was that I was barely breathing. Without being conscious of it, I was holding my breath for long moments. After struggling through a few sessions, I realized that it was when I was holding my breath that I felt the most comfort. Those were the moments when I was thinking about our son. I was happy to hold my breath and would have held it even longer if I had had the strength. In those moments, I would think about life before the terrible night, and I would begin to think about what a pleasant relief not breathing would be.

Trying to even out my breathing created a dilemma that made me more anxious than ever. It was hard to think about wanting, really wanting things to get better because I wasn't yet sure I had what it would take to be here at all. In order to get better, I would have to learn how to breathe, but learning how to breathe might take me away from the intimate moments I had shared with our son. I did not want to leave him. The more the hospital staff encouraged me to deal with the anxiety, the more I felt I could let go and never bother coming back.

∘ Epiphany of Despair ∘

I had come face to face with the real problem. You see, I thought I was trying to get used to living without my son, when in fact I was trying to figure out whether I had it in me to continue to live at all. It was a very dark time for me as I struggled with the dilemma that death created. I was at war with myself. One side of me was saying, "You must somehow make it through; you must be prepared to do whatever it takes to continue to live, if not for yourself then for your husband and children." The other side was saying, "This pain will never go away and you are too weak to live with this much pain. Just stop it, however you must." I hated my family for making the decision so difficult. I hated God for putting me in the middle of this mess. I hated myself for being so pathetically weak.

All my life I had been taught to run from death, that death was the enemy and I must fight to keep it away; now death was with me both morning and night, like a secret lover, calling to me. I did not dare tell anyone how close death and I had become. I thought being preoccupied with death meant I was mentally ill and that all must be protected from it.

It was not until I heard others at the hospital talk about their secret that I began to see I had it all wrong. In my grief I had come to the wrong conclusion. Death was not mine. It did not belong to me. It had not come to seduce me. The intimacy I shared with these people helped me understand that death was with all of us. I realized that I was quite sane, that I was simply being honest in asking the big questions about life: Why would anyone decide to live if the outcome of living is eventually death? Why would anyone love, if the outcome of love is loss?

I had thought it was my question alone when in fact it is the question that all humans ask. Until I spent time on the psychiatric ward and met those courageous people, I did not know how intimately all humans were connected. Death lives at the heart of all who live. It does not sit on the outside. It does not come to only some. It connects all of us. All parents who have lost children. All children who have lost parents. All who have lost someone they love.

I had been focused on the uniqueness of my experience, looking for ways to make sense of what had happened to me and to my family. What I learned as I sat day after day and heard others talk about their sorrow and trauma was that the suffering we face with death is the price we pay for being human. I didn't set the rules for the game of life. Counting how long my son had lived, and whether his short life was fair, did not seem relevant in this setting. In fact, there was no counting here. There was no one who dared say that a mother who had lost a twenty-year-old son was more deserving than a woman who had lost her infant son;

or that an aging man who had lost his wife of fifty years was less deserving than a young widower; or that a child who was alone in the world ought not to miss his parents.

The palpable pain of humanity spoke for itself. Here we were all equal, the president of the big company, the young mother, and the biker with the tattoos: each one of us was confronted with the fact that death is real. Each one of us was faced with the question, can I, somehow, learn how to live with death, or must I throw up my hands and say I cannot accept living in a world where death is real? No one was excused from making a decision.

Each day I would sit, going over the question. The price of answering either way was beyond what I could pay. I went over and over it, hoping I had missed something, fearing that I had not. I was completely at a loss. So was everyone else.

◦ ACCEPTANCE ◦

The hospital staff did their best to join us in our thoughts, but they were not with us in the well. They were like rescue workers who had come to the top of the well and let down a ladder. They were saying to us, "Grab hold of the ladder and we will take you back to the land of the living. Let us help you rid yourself of your thoughts of death, so we can help you to rise out of the well of sorrow."

But they did not have the context that we had. They did not understand how complicated the whole thing was. They did not know how little we wanted to get away from this well. They did not know about the sorrow that death had caused and the desire we nevertheless had to embrace it in order to follow the ones we loved. They did not know that death was no longer an enemy; that it had become part of who we were. We could not simply grab hold of their ladder and leave death behind; to do so would mean being transported away from thoe ones we loved. It would mean pretending we did not know the truth about life, or the truth about the suffering that remained.

It seemed to me that I had come upon two different worlds. The first was the one from the past where I had lived with my family before my son was killed: one where on occasion we talked about the need for life insurance but had never got around to doing anything about it. The second world was here in the well: a place where there was no escaping the fact that the natural outcome of life is death. In the world away from the well, I had been surrounded by people who did not know death; the world I lived in now was dominated by thoughts of death.

The two worlds did not seem to fit together. Out of the well, I was an accomplished reporter, always ready to go the distance to get at the root of the problem. In the well, I was stuck wandering around in circles, always ending up with the same question, can I learn how to live with the knowledge that death is real?

Two worlds: one asked me to pretend that there was no question; the other demanded an answer.

It was as I was trying to define the nature of these two separate worlds that I began to get better. You were smart, I told myself. You have taken on some daunting tasks in the past. Maybe there is a way to investigate these two worlds. After that you can make your decision. As I tried to categorize people's experience, I began to see I had it wrong. People could not be separated into two worlds. It was not as simple as those who knew death and those who did not know death. Everyone at some point in their lives would travel from one world to the other. We are all — always — in transition between the two worlds.

I had been thinking about whether I had it in me to go back to the world without my son; now I was beginning to think, what if I could learn to effectively commute between these two contrasting worlds? What if there was a way for me to learn to go back to being a wife and mother to my family, without leaving our dead son?

I began to reflect on the world of grief I was living in. Here in the hospital I had the support of a community that understood my suffering: people who were wide awake to the facts about life and death. But there was no food here, no light here, no hope for the future, no way for us to feed each other. In the well of grief, I was able to indulge myself with memories of our dead son but was too depleted to help my husband or our children. I could simply exist and remember. In this place of death I could not help anyone.

∘ ACQUIRING RESOURCES — SELF, OTHERS, GOD ∘

It was an interesting time of negotiation. I was coming to the conclusion that I would have to try to leave the well of grief, but I did not yet know how I was going to manage that journey. It was not that I wanted to go off and try to live differently. It was simply that I decided I must do so.

I committed to learning how to take care of myself for the journey I was about to take, even though at the time I didn't know what that entailed. I had to learn how to breathe again without holding my breath. I had to tell myself to put one foot in front of the other. I had to learn how to restore the rhythm of life by listening to music and moving my body. I had to learn to truly be with my husband again, not solely out of sympathy or need. We had to learn to be with each other.

I remember walking away from the hospital. I felt as though I was going to fall right off the edge of the earth. Marc walked beside me with an absolute sense of purpose, his body as stiff as mine. Neither of us was sure we could manage. We both knew it was time to try. I thought first about myself, but when I could feel the pain emanating from his body, I thought about him. I looked into his face and I could see the fear. I reached over and took his hand. We grasped each other tighter with each step we took. There were jobs to be done, obligations to keep. I thought about trying to go in to work alone, but I wasn't sure I was strong enough to face the looks of pity that would greet me. I knew it would be equally hard for Marc.

We decided we could run interference for each other. I went to work with him; he came to work with me. I sat in a corner of his office for several weeks, and he sat in a corner of mine. I don't remember whether we even talked to each other during those times, but the physical presence of someone who understood was enough to keep me on my way. The children scoffed at how we babysat each other, but we were teaching them not to overestimate how difficult it is to learn to live again. It was important to use each other as a resource.

While I was learning to live with my son's death, I thought death had taken over my entire world. Now I know that I have always lived in a world that includes death. Death is not an enemy that comes from another place; it is part of who we are as humans. Death is part of the one world that each one of us lives in.

Because of my own grief, I have developed a kinship with those who know suffering and a deep sense of empathy for those who have yet to learn. When I look into the eyes of someone who is in pain, I must respond to their suffering.

I have become a guide. I bring knowledge from those who suffer to those who do not yet know. I bring food and shelter to those who find themselves burdened with the weight of grief, so that when they are strong enough to begin their learning, I can help teach them how to acquire the resources they will need to begin their own journey. If they are not able to travel alone, then I try to find them someone to help.

This is where you in the healing professions come in. It is not your job to get people out of the well by lowering the ladder and encouraging them to climb up and never look back. It is your job to travel down into the well and give them comfort and help to guide them as they develop their own process. You must walk with them as they learn to create their own path — from the past, to the present, to the future. Each step of their journey marks a link that joins their two worlds.

In understanding death I have created a pathway to living. It is living life to the fullest that has made the reality of death less threatening. Coming back to the well now is like going back to the place of my birth: the place where I began to truly understand the reality of the world. My time in the community of those who have suffered loss fills me up. It is like having a great meal that allows me to go without food for long stretches of time. It is what gives me strength to continue to live, to enjoy life. It is where I am reminded of the need to be humble. I have learned to bring hope to the people who find themselves at the bottom of the well. They in turn have nourished my soul. My own suffering has become the source of my compassion.

I have spent many years negotiating with my God. We have had many conversations. Have I forgiven God? I am not sure that I have always been God's friend. What I can say is that I have chosen to be a forgiving person. I have chosen to accept that there may be things I do not understand. I have chosen not to spend my time here thinking about retribution. I have been too busy.

And now as I approach old age, what I can say is, I have done my job; I have stayed and lived. I have used my time wisely and soon it will be time for me to go. You see, death is not my enemy. It is death that will take me to my son.

CLOSING COMMENTS

In closing, please allow me to suggest several points to be considered as we continue to examine death as it relates to life.

There is an identifiable process of learning to live with death.
The stages of this process are **Surviving**; **Assessing** — Self, Others, God; **Depression**; **Epiphany of Despair**; **Acceptance**; and **Acquiring Resources** — Self, Others, God. Those who go through this process must do a great deal of work at each stage, and it is the process as a whole that helps them learn to live with death. The process of reconciling grief leads to wisdom, understanding, and context as we apply meaning to life. I therefore call this the Grief Reconciliation Process.

The process clearly points out that the suffering of people facing death should not be compartmentalized into physical, mental, and spiritual components.
All aspects of a person are intertwined, and must be treated

simultaneously. Knowing this, we must reexamine the way we provide treatment to people who are learning to live with death. An interdisciplinary approach must be deployed. By mapping the stages of the Grief Reconciliation Process, we can start to mobilize the resources of various professional communities and encourage them to work together to help people at each stage of the process.

The process gives sufferers, families, and professionals a language with which to communicate.

This language helps identify the stage the sufferers are in and invites them to work their way through all of the stages. It can also help them realize that they do not have to carry their burden alone. There are others who are going through or have gone through a similar experience. It helps professionals determine how they can best help.

The language of grief reconciliation helps us discuss death as part of life. A bereaved mother recently told me that until she acquired this language, she felt that she was forced to choose between her own suffering and other people's discomfort when they asked her how many children she had. Having acquired new vocabulary and an understanding of the importance of educating people about grief, she began to answer, "I have three children, two of whom are living."

The development of this new language helps us reclaim death as part of life.

There is much to be learned about healthy living from those who have reconciled themselves to the reality of death as a natural part of life. At present, people who have had to learn to live with death describe themselves as being part of a secret club. However, as the stories in this book have helped us see, they are actually part of a club that *all* will eventually join. We must stop pathologizing grief. Death is part of who we are as humans.

The process invites us to take a whole new look at depression as it relates to the treatment of those who are dealing with death. The stories have shown us that people learning to live with death must come apart in order to come back together again in a whole new way. This can be unnerving for everyone involved. It is painful and frightening to see someone struggling and railing. Our impulse is to want to relieve them of the burden of their suffering. But we need to work alongside them as they work hard to gain context. Instead of pathologizing depression, we might be better served to see it as a stage where important work is taking place. Learning to live with death is hard and intense work, and our consistent support is a critical factor. As a community, we must examine how we offer support to those who are suffering. We must understand that without the right kind of support, they may become discouraged and give up on life.

The process invites theologians and spiritual leaders to understand the complexities of learning to live with death. It is important for them to see the spiritual needs of those they care for as intertwined with their physical pain and mental anguish. There is spiritual work to be done in each one of the stages. Conflicts with God ought not to be pathologized.

Those of us who work in the healing professions — physical, mental, and spiritual — must integrate an awareness of death into an overarching health promotion agenda.

There is much to be learned about healthy living from those who have reconciled themselves to the reality of death as a natural part of life.

My hope in sharing these stories is that we will begin to see the advantages of a deep exploration of our views of death. Living with the knowledge that death is real can help us develop ways to focus on what we deem to be important; how we want to live; and what we want to be remembered for.

While we often define ourselves, or are defined by others, by highlighting superficial differences, it is the things we hold in common that best define the community of mankind. We all share one world. We are born. We die. And in between we engage in the exquisite dance that we call the experience of being human. I hope this book will play a small role in your own journey of reflection and enlightenment.